PROMPT

PRactical Obstetric MultiProfessional Training

Course Manual

PROMPT

PRactical Obstetric MultiProfessional Training

Practical locally based training for obstetric emergencies

Course Manual

Edited by

Tim Draycott, Cathy Winter,
Jo Crofts and Sonia Barnfield

RCOG PRESS

Published by the **RCOG Press** at the Royal College of Obstetricians and Gynaecologists, 27 Sussex Place, Regent's Park, London NW1 4RG

www.rcog.org.uk

Registered charity no. 213280

First published 2008

ISBN 978-1-904752-55-4

RCOG Editor: Jane Moody
Design/typesetting: Karl Harrington
Index: Liza Furnival, Medical Indexing Ltd
Printed in the UK by Bell & Bain, 303 Burnfield Road, Thornliebank, Glasgow G46 7UQ

Contents

Contributors

Mr Valentine Akande	Consultant Obstetrician and Gynaecologist, Bristol
Dr George Attilakos	Specialist Registrar, Obstetrics, Bristol
Dr Sonia Barnfield	Specialist Registrar, Obstetrics, Bristol
Ms Christine Bartlett	Senior Midwife, Bristol
Dr Joanna Crofts	Specialist Registrar, Obstetrics, Taunton
Mr Mark Denbow	Consultant Obstetrician and Gynaecologist, Bristol
Dr Fiona Donald	Consultant Anaesthetist, Bristol
Mr Timothy Draycott	Consultant Obstetrician and Gynaecologist, Bristol
Ms Denise Ellis	Senior Midwife, Bristol
Mr David Evans	Consultant Neonatologist, Bristol
Dr Melanie Griffin	Specialty Trainee, Obstetrics, Bristol
Dr Shehrazad Halawa	Specialty Trainee, Obstetrics, Bristol
Prof Maureen Harris	Professor of Midwifery, Perth, Australia
Ms Alison Hodges	PROMPT Course Administrator, Bristol
Dr Judith Hyde	Consultant Obstetrician and Gynaecologist, Gloucester
Mr Mark James	Consultant Obstetrician and Gynaecologist, Gloucester
Dr Christina Laxton	Consultant Anaesthetist, Bristol
Ms Sharyn Mckenna	Clinical Risk Manager, Maternity, Bristol
Mr Fraser Mcleod	Consultant Obstetrician and Gynaecologist, Bristol
Mr Andrew McIndoe	Consultant Anaesthetist, Bristol
Dr Imogen Montague	Consultant Obstetrician and Gynaecologist, Plymouth
Ms Beverley Osborne	Senior Midwife, Bristol
Dr Alison Pike	Consultant Neonatologist, Bristol
Ms Sandra Reading	Head of Midwifery, Taunton
Mr Mark Scrutton	Consultant Anaesthetist, Bristol
Ms Deborah Senior	Senior Midwife, Bristol
Dr Dimitrios Siassakos	Specialist Registrar, Obstetrics, Bristol
Dr Thabani Sibanda	Clinical Research Fellow, Bristol
Dr Bryony Strachan	Consultant Obstetrician and Gynaecologist, Bristol
Dr Emma Treloar	Specialist Registrar, Obstetrics, Bristol
Dr Hannah Wilson	Specialist Registrar, Anaesthetics, Gloucester
Ms Cathy Winter	Practice Development Midwife, Bristol
Ms Stephanie Withers	Labour Ward Modern Matron, Bristol
Ms Elaine Yard	Senior Midwife, Bristol

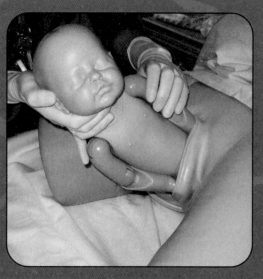

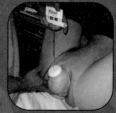

Acknowledgements

The PROMPT Foundation operates under the umbrella of the North Bristol NHS Charitable Trust. The course has been developed and produced with the support of:

■ Staff of North Bristol NHS Trust, UK
■ The South West Obstetric Network, UK
■ All researchers, facilitators and participants of the SaFE Study (DOH, UK)
■ Limbs & Things, Bristol, UK
■ Ferring Pharmaceuticals, UK (supported through an unrestricted educational grant)
■ UCB Pharma Ltd (support through an educational grant)

The final production of the PROMPT course would not have been possible without the invaluable help and support of:

■ The Louise Stratton Memorial Fund
■ Wendy and Mark Skuse
■ St Ursula's School, Bristol, UK

Royal College
of Midwives

Royal College of
Obstetricians and
Gynaecologists

List of abbreviations and terms

ABCD ....airway, breathing, circulation, displacement

AED ....automated external defibrillator

Algorithm ....A sequence of actions required to accomplish a task

ALS..................advanced life support

APH ....antepartum haemorrhage

APPT................activated partial thromboplastin time

AVPU ....alert, verbal, painful, unresponsive

BLS ....basic life support

BMI..................body mass index

BP....................blood pressure

Ca^{2+} ....calcium

CEMACH ....Confidential Enquiry into Maternal and Child Health

CESDI ....Confidential Enquiry into Stillbirths and Deaths in Infancy

cm ....centimetre

CO_2 ....carbon dioxide

CPR ....cardiopulmonary resuscitation

CT ....computed tomography

CTPA ....computed tomography pulmonary angiography

CTG.................cardiotocograph

CVA.................cerebrovascular accident

CVP ....central venous pressure

DIC ....disseminated intravascular coagulation

ECG.................electrocardiograph

EFM ....electronic fetal monitoring

FBC..................full blood count

FBS ....fetal blood sample

FHR..................fetal heart rate

FFP...................fresh frozen plasma

HELLP ....haemolysis, elevated liver enzymes, low platelets

HIV ....human immunodeficiency virus

IM....................intramuscular(ly)

IV.....................intravenous(ly)

ITU...................intensive therapy unit

IU ....international units

J ....joules

JVP ....jugular venous pressure

K^+ ....potassium

l........................litre

LFTs..................liver function tests

MAP ....mean arterial pressure

ml.....................millilitres

mmHg ....millimetres of mercury

mg...................milligrams

$MgSO_4$..............magnesium sulphate

mmol...............millimole

MRI..................magnetic resonance imaging

Na^+ ....sodium

NICE ....National Institute for Health and Clinical Excellence

O_2....................oxygen

$PaCO_2$...............partial pressure of carbon dioxide

PaO_2 ....partial pressure of oxygen

PEA..................pulseless electrical activity

pH ....hydrogen ion concentration

PPH..................postpartum haemorrhage

U&Es................urea and electrolytes

VF....................ventricular fibrillation

VT....................ventricular tachycardia

Course programme

Welcome to the PROMPT Course. This multiprofessional training course covers the management of a range of obstetric emergency situations. Each subject is presented in the following formats:

Interactive lectures based on the topics included in the course manual, with time for discussion and opportunities to draw from the participants' own clinical experience of actual emergency situations.

Interactive drills and **workshops** providing 'hands on' experience of practical skills and decision making in simulated obstetric emergency situations.

The course consists of the following modules:

- Team working
- Maternal collapse, including basic life support
- Severe pre-eclampsia and eclampsia
- Maternal cardiac arrest and advanced life support
- Intrapartum fetal monitoring, including CTG case reviews and National Institute for Health and Clinical Excellence guidelines
- Major obstetric haemorrhage
- Shoulder dystocia
- Cord prolapse
- Vaginal breech delivery
- Basic newborn resuscitation

Participants are expected to have read the course manual before they attend the training course and to have completed their CTG workbook.

A certificate of attendance will be given on completion of the PROMPT Course.

Module 1
Teamwork

Key learning points

- To understand the importance of good team working.
- To understand that effective communication is vital in emergency situations.
- To appreciate the different roles and responsibilities of members of a multiprofessional team.
- To understand the importance of shared decision making within the team.
- To recognise the value of being able to 'stand back and take a broader view' in an emergency situation.

Introduction

The most recent national Confidential Enquiry into Maternal and Child Health (CEMACH 2007)[1] has estimated that about half of all maternal deaths could be prevented with better care. While the report acknowledges that there has been no increase in the overall percentage of maternal deaths considered to have avoidable factors, the lack of multiprofessional team working and communication failures have once again been identified as contributory factors.[1,2,3] In addition, the Confidential Enquiry into Stillbirths and Deaths in Infancy (CESDI) has also identified poor communication and team working as a major contributor to fetal and neonatal mortality.[4,5] Both Enquiries have repeatedly recommended multiprofessional obstetric emergencies training for all staff providing care for mothers and babies. Annual drill training of all obstetric and midwifery staff is now mandated by the Maternity Clinical Negligence Scheme for Trusts – a UK NHS insurance scheme where maternity hospitals with a high standard of training, guidelines and audit are rewarded with reduced insurance premiums.[6] Similar recommendations have also been made in the USA.[7]

In 2000, Kohn[8] identified that healthcare teams are typically trained in separate professions with separate educational programmes. This results in the team members being less able to appreciate each other's strengths or recognise weaknesses, except in a crisis. The report recommends that: 'Patient safety programmes should establish interdisciplinary team training programmes – including the use of simulation for trainees and experienced practitioners'.[8]

Definitions

Teamwork is the combined effective action of a group working towards a common goal. It requires individuals with different roles to communicate effectively and work together in a coordinated manner to achieve a successful outcome.

Training has been defined as the systemic acquisition of knowledge (what we think), skills (what we do) and attitudes (what we feel) that leads to improved performance in a particular environment.[9]

Teamwork training

Conventional healthcare training has typically focused on specific, technically skilled tasks but with the increasing multiprofessional nature of healthcare provision, training in task-based skills alone may be inadequate. Multiprofessional team training may be necessary to further improve performance and outcome.[10]

Teamwork training is a key feature of most critical safety systems. The aviation industry trains cockpit and cabin crews in specific teamwork principles that are thought to be important to performance and safety. For example: preflight briefings, minimal disturbance during take-off and landing, using set phrases to alert other team members of a problem and identifying ways to overcome the inhibiting effect of hierarchy.[11] Many of these issues are also common to health care, yet formal teamwork training is rare.

Teamwork training applies the paradigm that people make fewer errors when they work in effective teams. Each member of the team can understand their responsibilities when processes are planned and standardised and team members can 'look out' for one another, noticing errors before they cause an accident.[12] In an effective multiprofessional team, members come to trust each other's judgements and attend to their safety concerns.

Improvements in outcomes

There is some early evidence to support training for obstetric emergencies in multiprofessional teams; most notably the association between improved obstetric and perinatal outcomes and the onset of clinical and/or teamwork training in one maternity unit in the UK and also a hospital in the USA.[13,14] The two training programmes associated with this improvement in outcome were set up and conducted 'in-house' and they trained 100% of staff. Both hospitals also reported the introduction of several infrastructural changes, often suggested by their staff after participating in the training. This, too, may have improved outcome.

A team is only as strong as its weakest link and so it is important that all staff providing care to mothers and babies are trained. In-house training appears to be the most efficient and cost effective means of training all staff in an institution. It can also address specific local issues and can be used as a driver for system changes.[13] It is easier to reinforce the key learning points of training if they become part of the ethos of the institution. Thus, training within the local environment may be the most effective way of improving outcomes.

Unfortunately, poor obstetric outcomes cannot always be prevented but, in many instances, the management of obstetric emergencies can be improved through enhanced knowledge and training in multiprofessional teams. Some simple teamworking principles are outlined below.

Communication

Communication is the transfer of information and the sharing of meaning. Often, the purpose of communication is to clarify or acknowledge the receipt of the information. Communication is often impaired under stress. It is important to learn effective techniques that increase awareness and help overcome these limitations.

Five requirements for effective communication are:

1. **FORMULATED**
   Give a clear message. It should be succinct and not rambling. For example:

   > "Sarah Smith is having an eclamptic fit. Please could you fast bleep the obstetric emergency team and ensure someone brings the eclampsia box into the room immediately."

2. **ADDRESSED TO SPECIFIC INDIVIDUALS**
   Use names of staff and allocate appropriate tasks to an identified recipient.

   > "Liz and Susan (midwives), please can you help get Mrs Jones into McRoberts' position."

   > "Hazel (healthcare assistant), please could you document times and actions as they are called out, on this laminated pro forma. Thanks."

3. **DELIVERED**
   The message should be sent clearly, concisely and calmly:
   When the obstetric emergency team arrives in your room, say:

   > "Susan Jones is having a postpartum haemorrhage and has lost approximately one litre of blood. Her placenta has been delivered and appears complete, and she has an intact perineum. I have given her one dose of IM Syntometrine but her uterus still feels atonic."

   rather than:

   > "Oh dear, Susan has just had a really big baby and I gave her Syntometrine but she is bleeding, really, really heavily. Oh dear, please can someone help me."

4. **HEARD**
   Adequate volume used and repeated back:

   > "You want me to give 250 micrograms of carboprost intramuscularly straight away."

5. **UNDERSTOOD AND ACTED UPON**
   Meaning acknowledged and action performed:

   > "OK. That's 250 micrograms of carboprost given
   > intramuscularly at 15.30."

In addition, the use of nonverbal communication, including making eye contact with individuals, helps to prevent ambiguity and promotes a shared knowledge of intention. Improper terminology, inaudible communication, excess chatter and incomplete reports should be avoided.

Team roles and responsibilities

Team leadership involves providing direction, structure and support for other team members. The team leader is often the most senior obstetrician present but may be the midwifery coordinator or anaesthetist. It is essential that the team leader is nominated and accepted by the rest of the team as early as possible.

Team leaders vary in their level of expertise when involved in a particular emergency situation and also in their readiness to lead. The team leader requires a certain amount of competence; however, it is unlikely that they possess all the abilities of every team member present. Therefore, their role should be to coordinate the activities of the specialists within the team by communicating clearly and simply, delegating tasks appropriately and planning ahead. In addition, a good team leader, respects the expertise of each team member, is willing to listen and is open to criticism and constructive feedback. **Their primary concern should be the success of the team not the leader**.

Other members of the team should have their individual roles identified and agreed as early as possible. They should be mutually supportive, communicate clearly and give regular updates. They should avoid becoming fixated on minutiae and objectively review their own performance. Constructive, open responses from team members reinforce beneficial behaviours throughout the team.

Situational awareness – the bigger picture

Situational awareness is how we notice, understand and think ahead in a fast-paced, constantly changing situation. It is that 'gut instinct' or 'sixth sense' that makes an expert midwife, obstetrician or anaesthetist. It involves recognising and understanding important cues, anticipating problems and sharing them with the team so that shared decision-making and goals are achieved.

Three levels of situational awareness have been suggested.[15] These levels are listed below and include examples related to obstetric emergencies.

1. **NOTICE** (perceive):
   Awareness of the patient status, the team members' status and all available resources; anticipating potential errors by noticing cues and sharing decision making:

   > 'It is the evening labour ward 'board' hand over between the labour ward coordinator and the senior obstetrician on call. The labour ward is full and two of the women are very ill: one with severe pre-eclampsia and poor urine output and the other has had a 1000-ml postpartum haemorrhage and requires an examination under anaesthesia. In such circumstances, it is vital that both team members have an awareness of the serious problems that may develop. They can then anticipate and plan how to manage the cases and also consider which team members may be required to assist with the problems'.

2. **UNDERSTAND** (comprehend):
   Share information with the team, think what these cues and clues may mean, be aware of common pitfalls, re-evaluate/stand back at regular intervals, seek to engage other team members in decisions:

   > 'On review of all the cases on the labour ward, the midwife coordinator and the senior obstetrician identify that there are several complicated problems that need decisions and action. They are considering whether it may be wise to call in the consultant obstetrician for support and to assist with the management of these problematic cases.

Before they can make this decision, both the midwife and the senior obstetrician go to each room for a thorough review, requesting an update from each of the midwives providing care. They then seek the opinion of the anaesthetist to gain further information that may influence the actions to be taken'.

3. THINK AHEAD (project):
   Anticipate, plan and prioritise:

   'Having sought further information and also the opinion of other team members, the labour ward coordinator and the senior obstetrician are now able to identify potential problems and therefore prioritise the cases to formulate an action plan. Their ability to do this is based not only upon the information provided by the other team members but also on their own knowledge and previous experience. In this instance, they both agree that their first action should be to call in the obstetric consultant for support and guidance with the management of the complicated cases'.

   Situational awareness allows individuals to be 'ahead of the game'. Experienced clinicians usually have good situation awareness; they often pick up subtle cues, understand them and anticipate problems.

Recognising cues for loss of situational awareness

In extreme situations, however, people can sometimes enter 'fast time', whereby their capacity to reason is so severely impaired by the stress of the workload that they are no longer able to function interactively with the rest of the team. Characteristic signs of 'fast time' include:

- poor communication
- inability to plan ahead
- tunnel vision
- fixation on irrelevant issues (such as less than ideal equipment) or displacement activities such as unnecessary disputes with colleagues.

'Fast time' at its worst can cause even good team players to completely 'freeze up'.

Maintaining/regaining situational awareness

One suggested way of maintaining situation awareness is to adopt the advanced life support (ALS) philosophy of the 'non-participant' leader.[16] Try not to become engaged in practical tasks that can be undertaken by others. This allows the leader to take a step back and maintain a broader view of the unfolding crisis. Team leaders sometimes have difficulty doing this in practice because they often have the particular 'hands on' skills required to deal with the problem.

To regain control of a situation, the following strategies should be tried:

■ Take the 'helicopter view' – stand back to get the bigger picture.

■ Declare an emergency – you will engage everyone's attention and boost the available human resources.

■ Communicate clearly and simply.

■ Plan ahead.

■ Delegate appropriately.

Team working under pressure

Pressure situations give us the feeling that everything needs to be done immediately and so the tendency to rush increases. Rushing tasks under pressure increases the potential for making errors. Therefore a good team leader should try to manage the emergency at a steady but efficient pace.

When the England rugby football team won the 2003 World Cup, they trained under the philosophy of T-CUP – Thinking Clearly Under Pressure. This principle can also be applied to the management of any obstetric emergency.

What makes a good team member?
■ Good communicator
■ Good understanding and acceptance of own limitations
■ Awareness of environment and limitations of others
■ Assertive
■ Nonconfrontational but willing to challenge if necessary
■ Receptive to the suggestions of all other team members
■ Thinks clearly

> ### Teamwork key points
>
> ■ Good team working is important because poorly functioning teams are associated with patient harm.
>
> ■ Teamwork training may improve clinical outcomes.
>
> ■ Multiprofessional teamwork training should be available to and integral with standard clinical training for all the birth team.

References

1. Lewis G, editor. *Saving Mothers' Lives: reviewing maternal deaths to make motherhood safer 2003–2005. The Seventh Report of the Confidential Enquiries into Maternal Deaths in the United Kingdom*. London: CEMACH; 2007.

2. Lewis G, Drife J, editors. *Why Mothers Die 1997–1999. The Fifth Report of the Confidential Enquiries into Maternal Deaths in the United Kingdom*. London, RCOG Press; 2001.

3. Lewis G, editor. *Why Mothers Die 2000–2002. The Sixth Report of the Confidential Enquiries into Maternal Deaths in the United Kingdom*. London, RCOG Press; 2004.

4. Confidential Enquiries into Stillbirths and Deaths in Infancy. Focus Group – Shoulder Dystocia. In: *5th Annual Report*. London: Maternal and Child Health Research Consortium; 1996. p. 73–9.

5. Confidential Enquiries into Stillbirths and Deaths in Infancy. The '4 kg and over' enquiries. In: *6th Annual Report*. London: Maternal and Child Health Research Consortium; 1996. p. 35–47.

6. NHS Litigation Authority. *Clinical Negligence Scheme for Trusts Maternity Clinical Risk Management Standards*. London: NHSLA; 2007.

7. The Joint Commission. Preventing infant death and injury during delivery. Sentinel Event Alert 2004;(30) [www.jointcommission.org/SentinelEvents/SentinelEventAlert/sea_30.htm].

8. Kohn LT, Corrigan JM, Donaldson MS. *To Err is Human: Building a Safer Health System*. Washington DC: National Academy Press; 2000.

9. Bloom BS, Krathwohl DR. *Taxonomy of Educational Objectives*. London: Longman; 1964.

10. Burke CS, Salas E, Wilson-Donnelly K, Priest H. How to turn a team of experts into an expert medical team: guidance from the aviation and military communities. *Qual Saf Health Care* 2004;13 Suppl 1:i96–104.

11. Helmreich R, Foushee H. Why crew resource management? Empirical and theoretical bases of human factors in training and aviation. In: Wiener E, Kanki B, Helmreich R, editors. *Cockpit Resource Management*. San Diego: Academic Press; 1993. p. 3–45.

12. Helmreich RL. On error management: lessons from aviation. *BMJ* 2000;320:781–5.

13. Sachs BP. A 38-year-old woman with fetal loss and hysterectomy. *JAMA* 2005;294:833–40.

14. Draycott T, Sibanda T, Owen L, Akande V, Winter C, Reading S, *et al*. Does training in obstetric emergencies improve neonatal outcome? *BJOG* 2006;113:177–82.

15. Endsley MR. The role of situational awareness in naturalistic decision making. In: Zsambok CE, Klien G, editors. *Naturalistic Decision Making*. New York: Lawrence Erlbaum Associates; 1997. p. 269–83.

16. Resuscitation Council (UK) Advanced Life Support Provider Course. General information [www.resus.org.uk/pages/alsgen.htm].

Further reading

Crofts J, Ellis D, Draycott T, Winter C, Hunt L, Akande V. Change in knowledge of midwives and obstetricians following obstetric emergency training: a randomised controlled trial of local hospital, simulation centre and teamwork training. *BJOG* 2007;114:1534–41.

Crofts JF, Bartlett C, Ellis D, Winter C, Donald F, Hunt LP, et al. Patient-actor perception of care: a comparison of obstetric emergency training using mannequins and patient-actors. *Qual Saf Health Care* 2008;17:20–4.

Royal College of Obstetricians and Gynaecologists, Royal College of Midwives, Royal College of Anaesthetists, Royal College of Paediatrics and Child Health. *Safer Childbirth: Minimum Standards for the Organisation and Delivery of Care in Labour*. London: RCOG Press; 2007.

Thomas EJ, Sexton JB, Helmreich RL. Discrepant attitudes about teamwork among critical care nurses and physicians. *Crit Care Med* 2003;31:956–9.

Module 2
Basic life support and maternal collapse

Key learning points

- Assessment and resuscitation of maternal collapse:
  - ☐ **A B C D**
  - ☐ 30-degree tilt.
- Calling for help – effective communication of problem to team.
- Equipment – know where to find emergency trolley, defibrillator, anaphylaxis box.
- Appropriate documentation.

Common difficulties observed in training drills

- forgetting to tilt mother
- not administering high-flow oxygen to mother
- not stating that it is a 'maternal cardiac arrest' when calling arrest team.

Introduction

Maternal collapse occurs in a variety of circumstances, ranging from an isolated and temporary drop in blood pressure to cardiac arrest and death. It is absolutely imperative that all healthcare professionals can provide basic resuscitation, regardless of the cause. Regrettably, in the most recent CEMACH Report (2007), resuscitation skills were considered poor in an unacceptably high number of the maternal deaths. The report recommends that all clinical staff should undertake regular training to improve basic, immediate and advanced life support skills.[1]

Basic life support algorithm

All healthcare professionals should be aware of the principles of basic life support. An outline of the basic life support algorithm is provided in Figure 2.1 but it is not intended to be a complete guide. Further information is available from the Resuscitation Council UK.[2]

What do we mean by maternal collapse?

Maternal collapse is severe respiratory or circulatory distress which may lead to cardiac arrest if untreated. Any of the vital observations in Box 2.1 should trigger an emergency response.

Box 2.1 Observations that trigger an emergency response	
Airway	Obstructed or noisy
Breathing	Respiratory rate less than 5 or more than 35 beats/minute
Circulation	Pulse rate less than 40 or more than 140 beats/minute
	Systolic blood pressure less than 80 or greater than 180 mmHg
Neurology	Sudden decrease in level of consciousness
	Decrease in Glasgow Coma Score of greater than 2
	Repeated or prolonged seizures

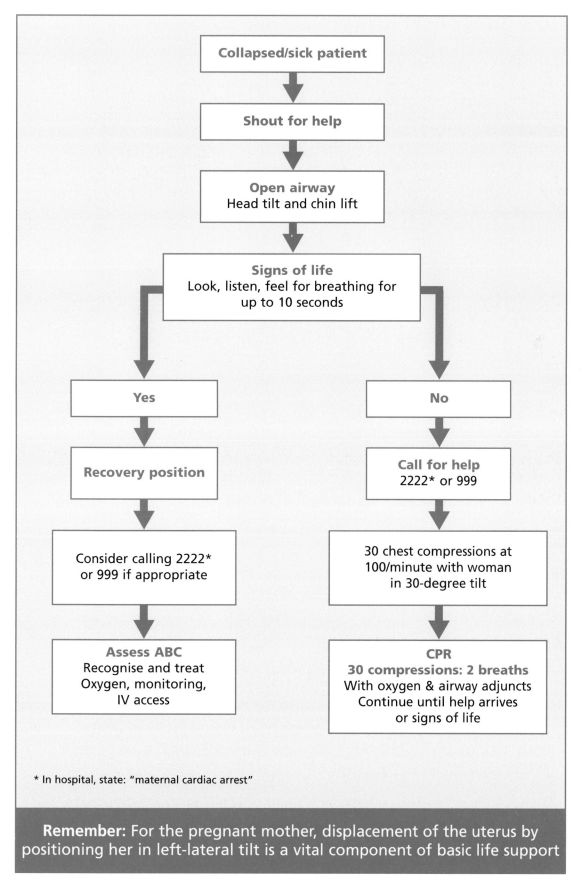

Figure 2.1 Basic life support algorithm

How do we deal with a maternal collapse?

The key to the effective management of maternal collapse is a simple and structured approach to diagnosis and treatment. The underlying principles of the management of any critically ill patient are the same and are often described through the ABCD approach (Airway, Breathing, Circulation, Displacement). Figure 2.2 illustrates a systematic way of diagnosing possible causes of maternal collapse. This, of course, should only be followed once initial stabilising ABC treatment has been commenced. The causes are discussed in more detail in the following sections.

Initial management

- Assess the responsiveness of the woman by gently shaking her and asking if she is all right. If there is no response, seek immediate help using the emergency bell, dialling 2222 in hospital or 999 if outside hospital.
- Turn her on to her back and support her in a left-lateral tilt using a pillow or wedge to reduce aortocaval obstruction.
- Open the airway using head tilt and chin lift manoeuvres.
- Assess breathing by looking at movement of the chest wall, listening for breath sounds and feeling for air on your cheek (look, listen, feel) for up to 10 seconds (beware of agonal breathing).
- While assessing breathing, observe for other signs of life, such as colour, movement.
- If there are no signs of life, commence basic life support (Figure 2.1) until help arrives (to provide advanced life support) or the woman shows signs of life.
- If the woman has signs of life, place her in the recovery position and give high-flow oxygen via a reservoir mask. Obtain intravenous access, take blood samples (full blood count, clotting screen, urea and electrolytes, glucose, liver function tests, group and save) and give intravenous fluids. Establish monitoring of vital signs with ECG, respirations, pulse, blood pressure measurement and pulse oximetry. Then perform a primary obstetric survey.

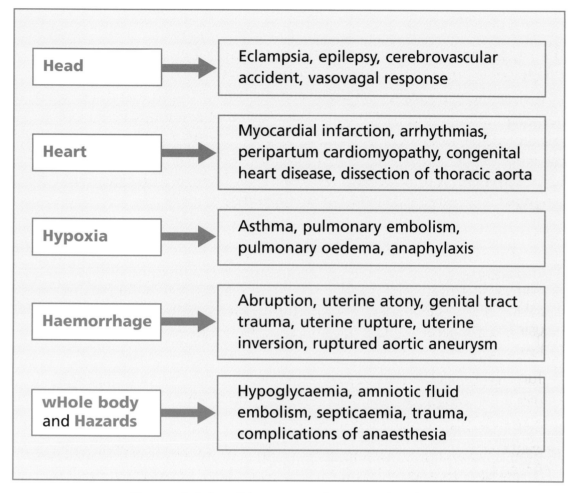

Head	Eclampsia, epilepsy, cerebrovascular accident, vasovagal response
Heart	Myocardial infarction, arrhythmias, peripartum cardiomyopathy, congenital heart disease, dissection of thoracic aorta
Hypoxia	Asthma, pulmonary embolism, pulmonary oedema, anaphylaxis
Haemorrhage	Abruption, uterine atony, genital tract trauma, uterine rupture, uterine inversion, ruptured aortic aneurysm
wHole body and Hazards	Hypoglycaemia, amniotic fluid embolism, septicaemia, trauma, complications of anaesthesia

Figure 2.2 Possible causes of maternal collapse

Primary obstetric survey

A primary obstetric survey should be performed in a logical manner, starting at the head and working downwards. This initial management should produce a working diagnosis and should enable treatment of the cause to commence. Box 2.2 shows the questions to be considered when performing the primary obstetric survey. It is important that senior obstetric and anaesthetic support is sought if not already present.

Box 2.2. Primary obstetric survey	
Head	How responsive is the patient? Is the patient fitting?
Heart	What is the capillary refill like? What is the pulse rate and rhythm? Is there a murmur?
Chest	Is there good bilateral air entry? What are the breath sounds like? Is the trachea central?
Abdomen	Is there an 'acute' abdomen (rebound and guarding)? Is there tenderness (uterine or non-uterine)? Is the fetus alive? Is there a need for a laparotomy or delivery?
Vagina	Is there bleeding? What is the stage of labour? Is there an inverted uterus?

Decide on continuing treatment

After the primary survey, the cause of the collapse and treatment required may be evident; for example, eclampsia or haemorrhage. If the cause is not obvious, only a few key treatment decisions are necessary.

1. Is fluid resuscitation a priority or is it contraindicated? If in doubt, fluid is usually beneficial: the exception is when the woman has, or is at great risk of, pulmonary oedema as may happen in severe pre-eclampsia or renal failure.

2. Is a laparotomy required for diagnosis or treatment? Is there evidence of an acute abdominal event? Does the fetus need delivery to aid resuscitation?

3. Is sepsis likely and are antibiotics therefore a priority?

4. Is intensive care needed to provide airway, respiratory or circulatory support?

Secondary obstetric survey

Further management is dependent upon the cause of the collapse. Once the woman has been stabilised, a secondary obstetric survey should be performed (Box 2.3).

Box 2.3. Secondary obstetric survey	
ACTION	DETAIL
History	Revisit the history of the collapse and the previous history of the woman
	Read the notes and ask the partner or relatives
Examine	Repeat the examination going from top to toe
Investigate	Take arterial blood gases, high vaginal swab, troponins, blood glucose, lactate, blood cultures, ECG, chest X-ray, and ultrasound of the abdomen
Monitor	Continue monitoring of ECG, respirations, pulse, blood pressure and pulse oximetry
Pause and think further	Consider further investigations such as CT/MRI scans and echocardiography
	Consider arterial and central venous pressure lines to aid monitoring
	Ask relevant experts for their opinions

Further key treatment decisions

Re-evaluate and continue to support the airway, breathing and circulation of the woman. Do you need intensive care to support?

Re-evaluate your working diagnosis at intervals to ensure the pattern still fits and treatment is working.

Specific causes of maternal collapse

Pulmonary thromboembolism

Pulmonary emboli are more common in pregnancy and the postpartum period, owing to the pro-coagulant effect of pregnancy and the mechanical obstruction of the abdominal uterus on venous return from the lower body. Pulmonary emboli may be small and nonsymptomatic or large and cause instant collapse and rapid death. Thromboembolism remains the most common cause of direct maternal death in the UK, with a rate of 1.94/100 000 maternities.[1]

Pulmonary emboli may present with shortness of breath, pleuritic chest pain or haemoptysis, or sudden collapse in a woman who may or may not have signs of a deep vein thrombosis. Clinical signs may include tachycardia, tachypnoea, hypoxia and evidence of right heart strain on ECG (S1Q3T3) with a raised jugular venous pressure. Diagnosis can be difficult; initial assessment and treatment should be made on symptoms and signs, plus arterial blood gases, ECG and chest X-ray with the diagnosis confirmed by ventilation–perfusion scanning (VQ scan) or computed tomography (CT) pulmonary angiography (CTPA).

Treatment should be supportive using facial oxygen, with ventilatory and cardiovascular support as necessary. Anticoagulation with heparin (subcuticular low molecular weight heparin or intravenous heparin) should be commenced on clinical suspicion of pulmonary embolism until the diagnosis is confirmed or refuted.

Haemorrhagic shock

Hypovolaemia, usually secondary to haemorrhage, is the most common cause of shock in obstetric patients. Signs of hypovolaemia include:

■ Tachycardia and tachypnoea

■ cold, pale skin

■ hypotension

■ reduced urine output

■ altered level of consciousness

■ narrowed pulse pressure (less than 35 mmHg difference between systolic and diastolic readings).

Prompt resuscitative fluid replacement is essential. If there is significant haemorrhage, arterial and central venous pressure (CVP) lines are often useful adjuncts for monitoring. The cause is most commonly obstetric in nature (such as uterine atony, abruption, ruptured uterus) but non-obstetric causes should also be considered.

Although rare, aneurysm rupture may occur (such as aorta, renal, splenic, iliac). This is often not recognised but is identified as a cause of maternal mortality in the Confidential Enquiries.[1] Urgent laparotomy should be considered when there are signs of an acute abdomen in conjunction with hypovolaemia.

Eclamptic convulsions and coma

Eclamptic convulsions and coma may resemble amniotic fluid embolus syndrome but the presence of hypertension, proteinuria and oedema in the eclamptic woman differentiates these two conditions. For more information about diagnosis and treatment, refer to **Module 3**.

Cerebrovascular accident

Cerebrovascular accidents (CVA) can present with any manner of neurological signs. CVA can be embolic or haemorrhagic in origin. Raised blood pressure, for example in severe pre-eclampsia, is a risk factor for CVA and any pregnant woman with systolic blood pressure of 160 mmHg or greater requires antihypertensive treatment to reduce the risk of a CVA.[1] Migrainous attacks can mimic CVAs. A CT or MRI scan should aid in the diagnosis and direct treatment.

Septicaemic shock

Signs of a fever, a history of 'flu-like' illness, 'hot and cold' symptoms with offensive lochia/liquor/discharge should be noted. Breathlessness, abdominal pain, diarrhoea and vomiting are all common symptoms which can mimic pneumonia and gastroenteritis. A flat red rash over large areas of the body with or without a history of sore throat should point towards a group A streptococcal (puerperal) septicaemia. Other common organisms are Gram-negative rods. Early antibiotics (high-dose cefuroxime and metronidazole) and supportive measures are needed. Look for signs of necrotising fasciitis.

The management of severe systemic sepsis, especially when accompanied by septic shock, remains a challenge to all those involved in the care of the critically ill pregnant woman. The onset of severe sepsis can be alarmingly rapid and, once established, it is difficult to treat. CEMACH (2007) has recommended the use of a sepsis resuscitation bundle, developed by the Surviving Sepsis Campaign.[1,3] The evidence-based care bundles cover resuscitation and management of severe sepsis. The resuscitation care bundle recommends that serum lactate, blood gases and blood cultures should be measured early in suspected cases of systemic sepsis. Fluid resuscitation should be prompt and its effect immediately noted.

> A failure of the woman to respond to 20 ml/kg of intravenous fluids should trigger an urgent critical-care referral.

Liaison with microbiology staff is important. In addition to blood cultures, a comprehensive infection screen (high vaginal swab, liquor, placental swabs, urine, sputum) should be undertaken. This will help to guide treatment with the most appropriate antibiotics.

Disseminated intravascular coagulation

Disseminated intravascular coagulation (DIC) can occur secondary to massive bleeding, severe infection, amniotic fluid embolism or anaphylaxis. When DIC occurs, there is an excessive consumption of platelets and clotting factors, resulting in a prolonged clotting time, low platelets, low fibrinogen and haemorrhage. Spontaneous bleeding may be noticed from needle puncture, intravenous cannulae or epidural sites. Vaginal haemorrhage may also occur, as may bleeding from the mother's gums.

Early involvement of haematology, senior obstetric and anaesthetic staff, as well as intensive care, is vital if DIC is suspected. Blood should be sent for full blood count, cross matching, clotting, fibrinogen and D-dimers. Haematology should advise on the appropriate blood products required to correct clotting. The cause of DIC should be investigated promptly and treated appropriately.

Hypo- or hyperglycaemia

Women with diabetes may collapse into a hypoglycaemic coma. Although rare, type 1 diabetes mellitus may commence in pregnancy. Blood glucose should always be tested in a collapsed woman if the cause is not obvious, and urine should be tested for the presence of ketones if diabetic ketoacidosis is suspected. Acute fatty liver may also present with maternal hypoglycaemia. If blood glucose is found to be below 3 mmol/l, 50 ml of 10% glucose solution should be administered intravenously.

Acute heart failure

Cardiac disease is the most common cause of indirect maternal death, as well as the most frequent cause of maternal death overall.[1] A known history of cardiac disease, chest pain with ECG changes or a new cardiac murmur may help to establish the diagnosis. If chest pain is a presenting feature then troponin levels should be taken 12 hours after the onset of pain. If cardiac ischaemia is suspected, 300 mg aspirin should be given orally unless contraindicated. If cardiac failure is suspected or there is a new murmur on auscultation, then urgent senior medical review and echocardiography should be arranged.

Pulmonary aspiration of gastric contents

Pregnancy increases the risk of pulmonary aspiration of gastric contents. This is because of progesterone-induced relaxation of the oesophageal sphincter and delayed stomach emptying, a problem which becomes more pronounced during labour. Aspiration is most likely to occur in the unconscious obstetric patient (for example, during induction or emergence from general anaesthesia) owing to the loss of the cough reflex. Gastric aspiration may present with coughing, cyanosis, tachypnoea, tachycardia, hypotension or pulmonary oedema.

Anaphylactic or toxic reaction to drugs or allergens

Anaphylactic or toxic reaction to drugs or allergens may present as convulsions or collapse. The close timing of administration of the drug or allergen (such as latex) in relation to the collapse may be indicative an anaphylactoid or toxic reaction.

Severe anaphylaxis should be treated with:

✔ oxygen 100% via non-rebreather mask

✔ IM adrenaline (epinephrine) 500 micrograms (1:1000) IM (into side of thigh), every 5 minutes, up to a maximum of two doses if necessary

✔ **OR** if an anaesthetist is present, up to 1 mg IV adrenaline (at a concentration of 1 in 10 000). Adrenaline should be diluted to a concentration of 100 micrograms/ml (1 mg in 10 ml) and then given in 0.5-ml aliquots as required.

✔ prepare other drugs: chlorpheniramine 10–20 mg IM/IV; hydrocortisone 100–500 mg IM/IV; nebulised salbutamol 2.5–5.0 mg; crystalloid/Haemaccel® (KoRa)/Gelofusine® (Braun) 1–2 litres IV.

Amniotic fluid embolism

Although a rare and largely unavoidable condition, there has been an apparent and inexplicable rise in maternal deaths from amniotic fluid embolism as reported by CEMACH (2007), with a rate of 0.8/100 000 maternities. The condition occurs when amniotic fluid enters the maternal circulation and causes maternal collapse, often leading to cardiac arrest. The woman is often conscious at the onset of symptoms. Presentation is acute with shivering, sweating, anxiety and coughing, followed by respiratory distress and cardiovascular collapse (hypotension, tachycardia and possible arrhythmias). DIC can quickly develop, causing massive maternal haemorrhage.

Diagnosis must initially be presumptive. Treatment involves supporting the respiratory and cardiovascular systems and correction of clotting abnormalities. Early liaison with haematology staff is vital.

If the woman survives, diagnosis can be confirmed by identification of vernix, fetal hair or fetal squames from the maternal right-sided circulation. Fetal squames have been recovered in the maternal sputum in some cases. The presence of pulmonary hypertension may also be demonstrated.

Air embolism

An air embolism may occur following a ruptured uterus, during administration of intravenous fluids or blood products under pressure, or following manipulation of the placenta at caesarean section. It is associated with chest pain and collapse. An important differentiating factor from amniotic fluid embolism is the auscultation of a typical waterwheel murmur over the praecordium.

References

1.   Lewis G, editor. *Saving Mothers' Lives: reviewing maternal deaths to make motherhood safer 2003–2005. The Seventh Report of the Confidential Enquiries into Maternal Deaths in the United Kingdom.* London: CEMACH; 2007.

2.   Resuscitation Council (UK) [www.resus.org.uk].

3.   Surviving sepsis Campaign [www.survivingsepsis.org].

Further reading

Marx GF. Cardiopulmonary resuscitation of late-pregnant women. *Anesthesiology* 1982;56:156.

Oates S, Williams GL, Res GAD. Cardiopulmonary resuscitation in late pregnancy. *BMJ* 1988;297:404.

Schaerf RHM, DeCampo T, Avetta J. Haemodynamic alterations and rapid diagnosis in a case of amniotic fluid embolus. *Anesthesiology* 1977;46:155.

Whitty JE. Maternal cardiac arrest during pregnancy. *Clin Obstet Gynecol* 2002;45: 377–92.

Ziadlourad F, Conklin KA. Amniotic fluid embolism. *Semin Anesth* 1987;6:117–22.

Module 3
Pre-eclampsia and eclampsia

Key learning points

- To manage an eclamptic fit effectively, including drug administration.
- To understand the care and monitoring of a woman being treated with magnesium sulphate.
- To understand the risk factors and recognise the signs and symptoms of severe pre-eclampsia.
- To understand the potential complications of severe hypertension, and to become familiar with the equipment and medication used in the management of severe hypertension.
- The importance of detailed contemporaneous documentation.

Common difficulties observed in training drills

- Not calling for help.
- Not stating the problem clearly.
- Not performing basic resuscitation.
- Incorrect administration and labelling of magnesium sulphate.
- Failure to restrict fluids.
- Failure to stabilise the woman before delivery.

Introduction

The Confidential Enquiries have reported a steady decline in maternal deaths related to pre-eclampsia and eclampsia in the United Kingdom, with a current mortality rate of 0.85 per 100 000 maternities.[1,2] Despite this encouraging reduction in rate, substandard care is still a problem, and the most recent report again identifies the need for adequate recognition of the severity of the disorder and also effective treatment.

Pre-eclampsia

Pre-eclampsia is a multi-system disorder of pregnancy characterised by hypertension and proteinuria with or without peripheral oedema. It is a disorder of the vascular endothelial function specific to pregnancy and is thought to arise in the placenta as a result of ischaemia.

Pre-eclampsia is one of the most common underlying causes of maternal and perinatal mortality (Box 3.1) and occurs in 3% of pregnancies. In developing countries it accounts for 50 000 maternal deaths annually.[3]

Box 3.1. Maternal complications of pre-eclampsia

Placental abruption

HELLP syndrome (characterised by haemolysis, elevated liver enzymes and low platelets)

Disseminated intravascular coagulation

Renal failure

Intracranial haemorrhage

Eclampsia

Coma

Acute respiratory arrest

Pre-eclampsia may also affect the fetus. There is a risk of intrauterine growth restriction, oligohydramnios, hypoxia from placental insufficiency or placental abruption, and premature delivery. Predisposing risk factors for pre-eclampsia are shown in Box 3.2.

> ## Box 3.2. Predisposing risk factors for pre-eclampsia
>
> **Nulliparity**
>
> **Essential hypertension**
>
> **Diabetes**
>
> **Multiple pregnancy**
>
> **Maternal age (extremes of maternal age)**
>
> **Previous pre-eclampsia**
>
> **Family history of pre-eclampsia**

Eclampsia

Eclampsia is defined as one or more convulsions in association with pre-eclampsia. Forty-four percent of seizures occur postpartum, 38% antepartum and 18% intrapartum. The recurrence rate of seizures is 5–20%, even with treatment.

In the UK, the incidence of eclampsia is 2.6/10 000 maternities as surveyed through the UKOSS system.[4] This represents a significant decrease since a previous national surveillance study, which found an incidence of 4.9/10 000 maternities.[2] There is a high rate of maternal complications associated with eclampsia, with at least one major morbidity in 35% of cases. Neurological complications may include coma, focal motor deficits and cortical blindness and cerebrovascular haemorrhage is a complicating factor in 1.2% of cases.[5]

Presenting features

Eclampsia presents as tonic clonic seizures, with jerking limb and head movements. The mother may become cyanosed. Tongue biting or urinary incontinence may occur. Most seizures are self-limiting and usually resolve within 90 seconds; however, eclampsia can be a very frightening experience for both family members and staff.

Management of eclampsia

The management of eclampsia involves basic life supportive measures as well as management of seizures. An outline for the initial management of eclampsia is shown in Figure 3.1. Management is described in more detail in the next section and is followed by details of the severe pre-eclampsia guidelines. Hypertension treatment guidelines are provided in the final section.

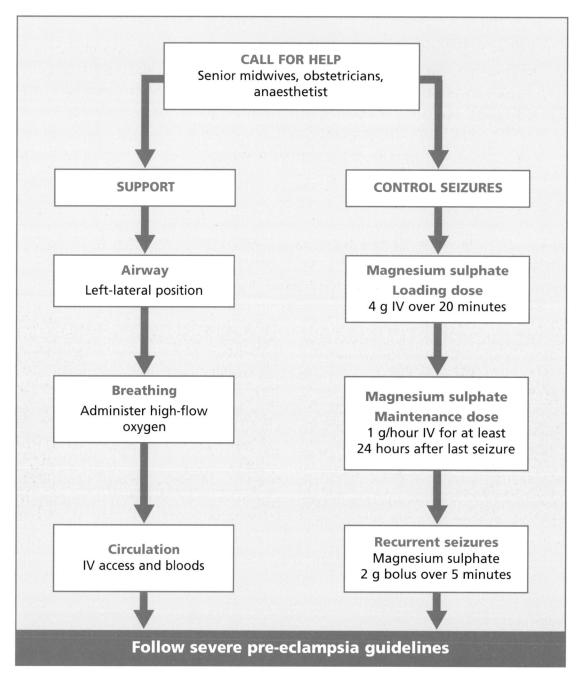

Figure 3.1 Outline of the initial management of eclampsia

Call for help

Ring the emergency buzzer to summon help. This includes calling for a senior midwife, the most experienced obstetrician available and an anaesthetist. Contact the consultant obstetrician and consultant anaesthetist.

■ Note the time the seizure occurred and its duration.

■ Note the time of the emergency call and time of arrival of staff.

Support – airway, breathing, circulation

Remember that most seizures are self-limiting. Remain calm. Monitor and maintain airway, breathing and circulation as your first priority. Give high-flow facial oxygen by facemask with a reservoir bag. Move the mother into the left-lateral position and protect her from injury. Do not attempt to restrain her during the fit. Immediately following the fit, ensure the woman is maintained in left lateral with an open airway.

Eclampsia box

Many units will have an emergency box containing a laminated treatment protocol as well as the emergency equipment and medication required for the immediate management of eclampsia (Figure 3.2).

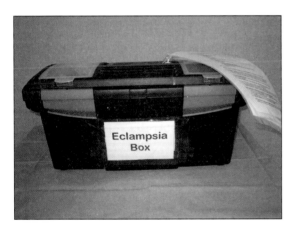 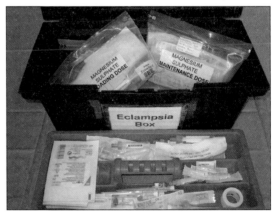

Figure 3.2 Eclampsia box with laminated treatment algorithm attached and showing contents

Control of seizures

Site a large bore intravenous cannula and take bloods for full blood count, urea and electrolytes, liver function tests, clotting and group and save. Start treatment with magnesium sulphate.

Magnesium sulphate emergency protocol

Loading dose: 4 g magnesium sulphate over 20 minutes

- Draw up 8 ml of 50% magnesium sulphate solution (4 g) followed by 12 ml of 0.9% saline (physiological) into a 50-ml syringe.
- This will give a total volume of 20 ml.
- Place the syringe into a syringe driver and run it at 60 ml/hour.
- The IV infusion will run in over 20 minutes.

Maintenance dose: 1 g/hour

- Draw up 20 ml of 50% magnesium sulphate solution (10 g) followed by 30 ml of 0.9% saline into a 50-ml syringe.
- This will give a total volume of 50 ml.
- Place the syringe into a syringe driver and run it at 5 ml/hour.

> Remember to reduce the infusion rate when changing from the loading dose to the maintenance dose.

- Continue infusion for 24 hours following the last seizure.

Recurrent seizures while on magnesium sulphate

- Seek immediate senior help.
- Draw up 4 ml of 50% magnesium sulphate solution (2 g) followed by 6 ml of 0.9% saline into a 10-ml syringe.
- This will give a total volume of 10 ml.
- Give as an IV bolus over 5 minutes.
- If possible, take blood for magnesium level prior to giving the bolus dose.

> The maternal condition should always take precedence over the fetal condition.
> The mother should be stabilised before delivery.

The results of the Collaborative Eclampsia trial demonstrated that women treated with magnesium sulphate have fewer recurrent seizures compared with women treated with diazepam or phenytoin.[6] Magnesium sulphate appears to act primarily by relieving cerebral vasospasm.[7] The intravenous route is preferable because intramuscular injections are painful and complicated by local abscess formation in 0.5% of cases.

The subsequent MAGPIE Trial demonstrated that magnesium sulphate can prevent eclampsia (although the number of women needing treatment to prevent one woman having an eclamptic fit is large, particularly in the developed world).[8]

If further seizures occur, treatment with diazepam, phenytoin or thiopentone or propofol (if an anaesthetist is present) should be considered. Consider other causes of seizures, such as intracranial haemorrhage and the use of cranial imaging with CT, MRI or magnetic resonance venogram.

Magnesium sulphate is excreted in the urine by the kidneys. Magnesium toxicity is unlikely if standard doses are given and the woman has a normal urine output and therefore the measurement of levels is not necessary. However, if the woman is oliguric or has renal impairment, magnesium levels are more likely to rise, causing toxicity. In these circumstances, it is advisable to administer the loading dose only. At toxic levels, there is loss of deep tendon reflexes, followed by respiratory depression, respiratory arrest and ultimately cardiac arrest. If maternal collapse occurs, follow the emergency protocol in Box 3.3. If toxicity is suspected, stop the magnesium sulphate infusion and take blood for magnesium levels.

Box 3.3. Magnesium sulphate emergency protocol

CARDIOPULMONARY ARREST ON MAGNESIUM SULPHATE

- Stop magnesium sulphate infusion

- Start basic life support

- Give 1 g calcium gluconate IV (10 ml of 10% solution) over 10 minutes

- Intubate early and ventilate until respiration resumes

Severe pre-eclampsia management guidelines

Severe proteinuric pre-eclampsia where the decision to deliver has been made: criteria for administering prophylactic magnesium sulphate

■ Hypertension ≥ 160/110 mmHg and protein ≥ +++

■ Hypertension ≥ 150/100 mmHg with proteinuria (≥ 0.3 g/day or ≥ ++) and at least one of the following:

  ☐ headache, visual disturbance, epigastric pain

  ☐ clonus ≥ three beats

  ☐ platelet count < 100 × 10^9/l

  ☐ ALT (alanine aminotransferase) > 50 iu/l

  ☐ creatinine > 100 micromol/l or creatinine clearance <80 ml/minute.

Note: Clinical discretion should be used to include women who present with atypical symptoms.[1]

Details of the management principles are outlined in Figure 3.3. These principles are discussed in more detail in the following section.

Management principles

The management of severe pre-eclampsia and eclampsia requires the initiation of complex treatment plans. Documented guidelines should be available and referred to by clinicians. Experienced medical and midwifery staff should provide individual care.

1. Stabilise

Effective and timely antihypertensive treatment is vital.[2]

Control of hypertension

In the latest triennial report on maternal deaths, the single major failing in critical care in deaths of women with eclampsia and pre-eclampsia was inadequate treatment of systolic hypertension resulting in intracranial haemorrhage.[2] The exact mechanisms that link hypertension with intracranial haemorrhage are still unclear, but systolic hypertension is

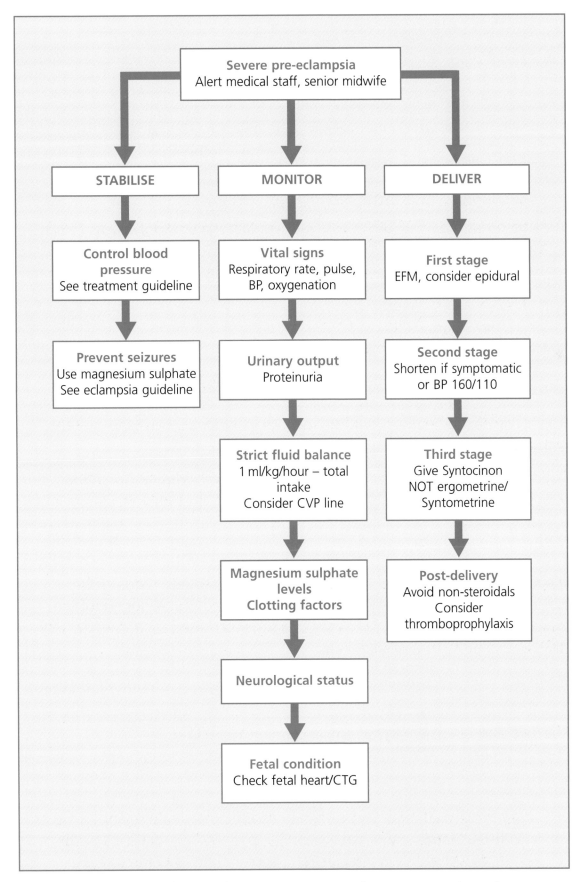

Figure 3.3 Outline of the management of severe pre-eclampsia

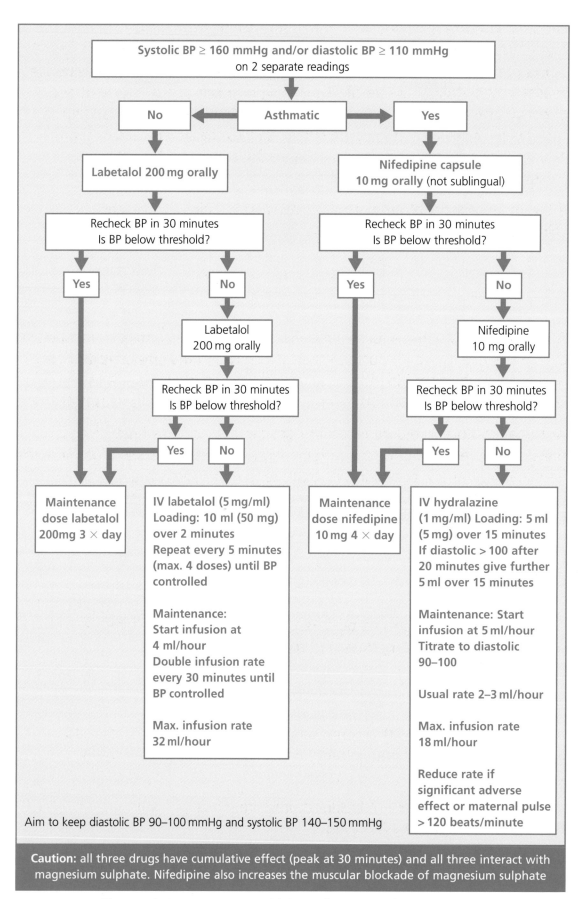

Figure 3.4 Treatment guidelines for severe hypertension

certainly important. In addition, mean arterial pressure (MAP) measurements may not always impart the real threat of a very high systolic blood pressure. The CEMACH Report suggests that based on the evidence available, a systolic pressure of 160 mmHg or more, requires urgent and effective anti-hypertensive treatment. It also identifies that pre-eclampsia can rapidly worsen, and in some circumstances, treatment at less than 160 mmHg, may be advisable (see Figure 3.4 for severe hypertension treatment flow chart).

If the mean arterial blood pressure values are required, these can be calculated using the formula below.

$$\text{MAP} = \text{Diastolic BP} + \frac{\text{Systolic BP} - \text{Diastolic BP}}{3}$$

Any prescribed antihypertensive medication should be continued in labour and at caesarean section (usually labetalol and/or nifedipine). Obstetricians and anaesthetists should also be aware of the hypertensive effects of laryngoscopy and intubation when administering a general anaesthetic.[2]

Automated blood pressure recording devices can underestimate blood pressure in pre-eclampsia to a serious degree. Blood pressure values should be compared at the beginning of treatment with those obtained by a manual device and an appropriately sized cuff should be used[10]. Consideration should be given to the use of an arterial line for difficult cases.

Prevent seizures

Magnesium sulphate should be given as for the previous eclampsia guideline; that is, loading dose and maintenance infusion.

2. Monitor

A mother's condition can deteriorate rapidly. Vigilant observation and assessment is required and should be recorded on a specialised high dependence chart.

- Respiratory rate, pulse and blood pressure – every 15 minutes until stabilised, then every 30 minutes.
- Hourly urine output – Foley's catheter with urometer.
- Hourly oxygen saturations.

■ Routine blood samples 12–24 hours: FBC, clotting screen, U&Es, LFTs.

Additional observations and investigation for mothers on magnesium sulphate:

■ Continuously monitor oxygen saturation.

■ Hourly respiratory rate.

■ Hourly deep tendon reflexes.

■ If loss of reflexes, stop infusion and check magnesium levels.

■ If level < 4 mmol/l or reflexes return, recommence infusion at 0.5 g/hour.

■ If oliguric, magnesium levels should be taken (less than 100 ml in 4 hours). Therapeutic range is 2–4 mmol/l.

Strict fluid balance

Close monitoring of fluid intake and urinary output is required. Previous Confidential Enquiries have highlighted the risk of fluid overload causing pulmonary oedema in women with severe pre-eclampsia.

The maximum fluid intake (a combination of intravenous and oral intake) should be 1 ml/kg/hour. This is often approximated to 85 ml/hour. Beware of dilute drug administration and excessive oxytocin, as this may inhibit urinary output.

All women with severe pre-eclampsia should have an indwelling urinary catheter, with a urometer for hourly urine measurement. All fluid input and output should be clearly documented on a high-dependency chart.

There is little rigorous evidence about the effects of either volume expansion or diuretic therapy for women with pre-eclampsia or eclampsia. The aim is to run 'dry', as women die from fluid overload but rarely from renal failure. Hartmann's solution (compound sodium lactate) will be the fluid of choice for most cases or blood replacement if necessary.

If there is persistent oliguria (less than 100 ml of urine over 4 hours) this requires careful management, as shown in Figure 3.5, and a central line should be considered. A central line may also be helpful to aid fluid management when there are added complications such as postpartum haemorrhage, as well as severe pre-eclampsia. The aim is to maintain a central venous pressure between 0 mmHg and 5 mmHg. Great caution should be exercised with fluid treatment if the central venous pressure is greater than 5 mmHg.

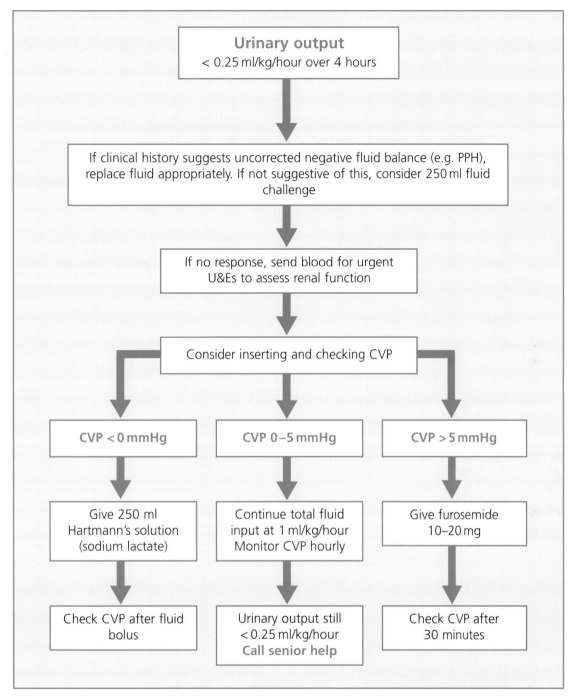

Figure 3.5 Fluid balance in the mother with oliguric pre-eclampsia

Clotting abnormalities

DIC is a potential complication of severe pre-eclampsia. Check activated partial thromboplastin time (APPT), prothrombin time and fibrinogen if platelet levels are less than 100×10^9. In addition, observe for clinical evidence of undue bleeding/bruises. If any of the investigations are abnormal, consider treatment with platelets and fresh frozen plasma (FFP) and liaise with the on call clinical haematologist (more information can be found in **Module 2**).

3. Deliver

Deliver the mother when her condition is stable. The choice of caesarean section or induction of labour should be made on an individual basis.

For the first stage of labour, close observation and the continuous attendance of an experienced midwife is required.

■ Use continuous electronic fetal monitoring: there is increased risk of fetal hypoxia and placental abruption.

■ Consider the use of epidural anaesthesia (pain tends to increase blood pressure).

It is safe for the mother to have a normal active second stage of labour provided that she does not have a severe headache or visual disturbances and that her blood pressure is within acceptable limits. Consider instrumental delivery if:

■ the mother complains of severe headache or visual disturbances

■ the blood pressure is uncontrolled (greater than 160 mmHg systolic or 105 mmHg diastolic, between contractions).

The third stage of labour should be managed with 5 units of Syntocinon® (Alliance) IM (or slowly IV).

> Ergometrine and Syntometrine® (Alliance) should not be given as these preparations may elevate the blood pressure further.

Post-delivery care

The mother will require continuous care after delivery. This may be for several hours or several days, depending on the circumstances. Remember that most eclamptic seizures occur in the postnatal period. Pre-eclampsia can worsen several days after delivery. If symptoms arise, monitor and investigate. This may occasionally mean transfer back to delivery suite.

Ensure adequate analgesia but note that nonsteroidals such as diclofenac must not be given, as this can precipitate renal failure.

Consider the need for thromboprophylaxis. Apply thromboembolic deterrent stockings as soon as possible. Commence low molecular heparin post-delivery provided that platelet count is greater than 100.

Transfer to intensive therapy unit

Previous Confidential Enquiries have highlighted that units should have documented procedures for the transfer of a mother to an intensive therapy unit.[1]

The indications for transfer include:

- renal failure not responding to guidelines and after discussion with renal physicians
- need for ventilation:
  - uncontrolled seizures after delivery
  - unconscious mother
  - pulmonary oedema not responding to conservative measures.

References

1. Lewis G, editor. *Why Mothers Die 2000–2002. The Sixth Report of the Confidential Enquiries into Maternal Deaths in the United Kingdom*. London, RCOG Press; 2004.

2. Lewis G, editor. *Saving Mothers' Lives: reviewing maternal deaths to make motherhood safer 2003–2005. The Seventh Report of the Confidential Enquiries into Maternal Deaths in the United Kingdom*. London: CEMACH; 2007.

3. Roberts JM, Villar J, Arulkumaran S. Preventing and treating eclamptic seizures. *BMJ* 2002;325:609–10.

4. Knight M, Kurinczuk JJ, Spark P, Brocklehurst P. *United Kingdom Obstetric Surveillance System (UKOSS) Annual Report 2007*. Oxford: National Perinatal Epidemiology Unit; 2007.

5. Douglas KA, Redmond CWG. Eclampsia in the United Kingdom. *BMJ* 1994;309:1395–400.

6. Eclampsia Trial Collaborative Group. Which anticonvulsant for women with eclampsia? Evidence from the Collaborative Eclampsia Trial. *Lancet* 1995;345:1455–63.

7. Naidu S, Payne AJ, Moodley J, Hoffman M, Gouws E. Randomised study assessing the effect of phenytoin and magnesium sulphate on maternal cerebral circulation in eclampsia using transcranial Doppler ultrasound. *Br J Obstet Gynaecol* 1996;103:111–16.

8. MAGPIE Trial Collaboration Group. Do women with pre-eclampsia, and their babies, benefit from magnesium sulphate? The Magpie Trial: a randomised placebo-controlled trial. *Lancet* 2002;359:1877–90.

9. Martin JN Jr, Thigpen BD, Moore RC, Rose CH, Cushman J, May W. Stroke and pre-eclampsia and eclampsia: a paradigm shift focusing on systolic blood pressure. *Obstet Gynecol* 2005;105:246–54.

10. Royal College of Obstetricians and Gynaecologists. *The Management of Severe Pre-Eclampsia/Eclampsia*. Green-top Guideline No. 10A. London: RCOG; 2006 [www.rcog.org.uk/index.asp?PageID=1542].

Further reading

Cunningham FG, Gant NF, Leveno KJ, Gilstrap LC III, Hauth JC, Wenstrom KD. *Williams Obstetrics.* 21st ed. New York: McGraw Hill, 2003. Chapter 24: Hypertensive disorders in pregnancy. p. 567–618.

Duley L. Magnesium sulphate for pre-eclampsia and eclampsia; the evidence so far. *Br J Obstet Gynaecol* 1996;101:565–7.

Ellis D, Crofts JF, Hunt LP, Read M, Fox R, James M. Hospital, simulation centre and teamwork training for eclampsia management: a randomised controlled trial. *Obstet Gynecol* 2008;111:723–31.

Gilbert WM, Towner DR, Field NT, Anthony J. The safety and utility of pulmonary artery catheterization in severe preeclampsia and eclampsia. *Am J Obstet Gynecol* 2000;182:1397–403.

Johanson R. Critical care management of severe pre-eclampsia. *Fetal Matern Med Rev* 1997;6:219–29.

Keiseb J, Moodley J, Connolly CA. Comparison of the efficacy of continuous furosemide and low dose infusion in pre-eclampsia/eclampsia-related oliguria in the immediate postpartum period. *Hypertens Pregnancy* 2002;21:225–34.

Kwok HM, Sheridan DJ. Meta-analysis of frusemide to prevent or treat acute renal failure. *BMJ* 2006;333:420.

Ashelby L, Winter C, Fox R. Fluid balance in pre-eclampsia: What we know and what we don't. In: Studd J, Lin Tan S, Chervenak F, editors. *Progress in Obstetrics and Gynaecology Volume 17.* Edinburgh: Churchill Livingstone; 2006. p. 125–40.

Shennan AH, Waugh JJS. The measurement of blood pressure and proteinuria. In: Critchley H, MacLean AB, Poston l, Walker JJ, editors. *Pre-eclampsia*. London: RCOG Press; 2003. p. 305–24.

Visser W. Intravenous hydralazine vs nifedipine in severe pre-eclampsia. *J Hypertens* 1995;13:791–5.

Walker J (2000). Severe pre-eclampsia and eclampsia. Clinical obstetrics and gynaecology 14. 57–71.

Walker JJ. Pre-eclampsia. *Lancet* 2000;356:1260–5.

Young PF, Leighton NA, Jones PW, Anthony J, Johanson RB. Fluid management in severe preeclampsia (VESPA): survey of members of ISSHP. *Hypertens Pregnancy* 2000;19:249–59.

Module 4
Maternal cardiac arrest and advanced life support

Key learning points

- Management of cardiac arrest using advanced life support (ALS) algorithm.
- Recall the causes of maternal cardiac arrest.
- Mother on 30-degree tilt.
- Prepare for perimortem caesarean section by 5 minutes.
- Document details of management accurately, clearly and legibly.

Common difficulties observed in training drills

- Concentrating on ALS and forgetting to do basic life support.
- Not tilting mother.
- Lack of understanding that perimortem caesarean section is primarily performed for maternal resuscitation.
- Not calling neonatal team for baby

Introduction

Maternal cardiac arrest is rare and survival is low because of the physiological changes present in late pregnancy that often hamper effective cardiopulmonary resuscitative efforts.

This module gives a brief outline of advanced life support but does not intend to be a complete guide to advanced resuscitation techniques. More information and specific training is available from the Resuscitation Council (UK)[1] and the European Resuscitation Council.[2] The aim of this module is to provide midwifery and obstetric staff with an initial overview of advanced life support in relation to the pregnant woman.

Possible obstetric causes of cardiac arrest during pregnancy and postpartum include:

- haemorrhage
- pre-eclampsia/eclampsia
- pulmonary embolism
- amniotic fluid embolism
- septicaemia
- total spinal anaesthesia.

These causes should be considered in addition to other causes of cardiac arrest in the non-pregnant woman (such as cardiac disease, substance abuse, anaphylaxis, trauma). Potentially reversible causes of cardiac arrest (the four Hs and the four Ts) are discussed later in this module.

Cardiorespiratory changes in pregnancy

In the supine position, pressure from the gravid uterus causes aortocaval compression. At term, the inferior vena cava is completely occluded in 90% of supine women, resulting in a decrease in cardiac stroke volume (the amount of blood pumped out with each contraction of the heart) of up to 70%. This has a significant effect on the cardiac output that can be achieved during cardiopulmonary resuscitation (CPR).

Aortocaval compression should be minimised by tilting the woman into a left-lateral position, using a wedge, the tilt on a theatre table, pillows or even rescuers' knees.[3]

If, after 5 minutes of effective CPR, resuscitation has not been successful, a perimortem caesarean section should be performed. This will immediately relieve the vena caval obstruction caused by the gravid uterus and improves survival rates for both mother and infant.[4–6]

> It is important to continue with CPR throughout the caesarean section procedure.

The pregnant woman at term has a 20% decrease in pulmonary functional residual capacity and a 20% increase in oxygen consumption. She therefore, becomes hypoxic more rapidly than the non-pregnant patient.[7] The enlarged uterus, together with the resultant upward displacement of the abdominal organs, decreases lung compliance during ventilation, which makes adequate ventilation during cardiac arrest difficult.

Pregnancy increases the risk of pulmonary aspiration of gastric contents. Early tracheal intubation reduces this risk. However, oxygenation of the patient always takes priority and prolonged attempts at intubation should be avoided.

Management of life support

An outline of the management of advanced life support is shown in Figure 4.1. This is described in detail in the next section. Events that need to occur during a maternal cardiac arrest are outlined in Box 4.1.

Role of the team leader

The team leader is usually a doctor on the cardiac arrest team, however, anybody trained in advanced life support can lead the arrest. The team leader should direct the rest of the arrest team and ensure their safety. This is best achieved by standing back, delegating specific tasks to members of the team and ensuring that clear commands are given. The team leader must consider any correctable cause of cardiac arrest and decide whether administering any other drugs (Table 4.1) may be beneficial.

In a maternal cardiac arrest it is important for the team leader (or any other members of the team) to ensure and state at 4 minutes into the arrest that the baby will need to be delivered in 1 minute if the woman has not been successfully resuscitated. The neonatal team will be required to resuscitate the baby and hence, it is important to call them as soon as a maternal arrest occurs, so they have time to prepare equipment.

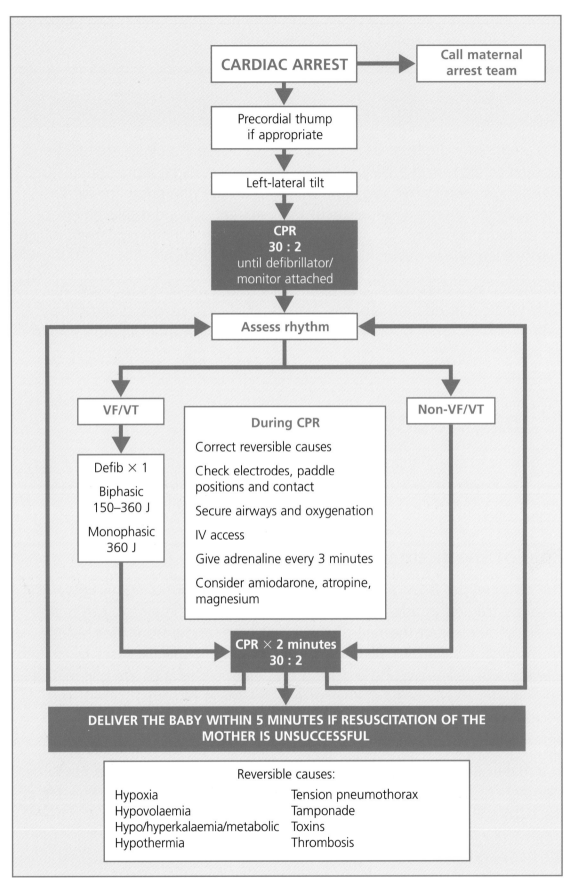

Figure 4.1 Adapted algorithm for the management of maternal cardiac arrest

Box 4.1. Management of maternal cardiac arrest

EVENT	ACTION
Help	■ Shout for help ■ **Ring 2222** state 'maternal cardiac arrest' and location of the incident ■ Ask for the arrest trolley, perimortem caesarean section pack and resuscitaire ■ **Call neonatal team (if pregnant woman)** ■ Ensure security doors are open so that arrest team can arrive ■ Contact blood bank and ask for emergency blood products ■ Phone haematology and biochemistry for urgent blood tests requested
Positioning	■ Lay the bed flat ■ Tilt the woman 30 degrees to the left ■ Move the bed into centre of the room ■ Take head end off the bed
Basic life support	■ If the arrest is monitored and witnessed, one precordial thump can be given ■ Open airway ■ Give 30 chest compressions (at rate of 100 compressions/minute) in middle of lower half of sternum to a depth of 4–5 cm ■ Next, give 2 breaths using a pocket mask or bag/mask ventilation ■ Continue at ratio of 30 chest compressions to 2 breaths (each breath lasting 1 second) until arrest trolley arrives
Equipment	■ **Defibrillator** – immediately apply gel pads and view rhythm to decide if a shock should be given ■ Deliver shock if appropriate ■ **Perimortem caesarean pack** from theatre – open in delivery room, attach blades, open sterile gloves ready to deliver baby at 5 minutes if CPR unsuccessful. Alert theatre team. ■ **Resuscitaire** must be turned on

cont.

Box 4.1. Management of maternal cardiac arrest (continued)

Investigations	■ **Large bore IV access** should be obtained as soon as possible
	■ **Venous blood** – send urgently for FBC, U&Es, LFTs, clotting screen, crossmatching, calcium and magnesium
	■ **Arterial blood gas** – some units may have blood gas analysers which will give immediate estimates of haemoglobin, K^+, Na^+, Ca^{++} and glucose as well as pH, paO_2 and $paCO_2$
Advanced life support	■ As soon as the arrest team arrives, a team leader should be appointed. In most hospitals a predetermined member of the arrest team assumes this role. They should coordinate the arrest including allocating specific tasks to members of the team
	■ CPR should be uninterrupted, except for shocks and rhythm checks (where appropriate), including during caesarean section, if required
	■ The anaesthetist will normally manage the airway/breathing
	■ **Shocks** – every 2 minutes if VF/ pulseless VT
	■ **Adrenaline** – 1 mg IV flushed with at least 20 ml water for injections. Repeated every 3–5 minutes
Deliver the baby	■ If resuscitation has not been successful by 5 minutes, deliver by emergency caesarean section
	■ **Continue CPR during operation**
	■ Ensure the neonatal team is in attendance.
Documentation	■ Note the time of the arrest, arrival of staff, timings of defibrillation, timing of drugs administered, time of delivery of baby and time cardiac output is regained

Table 4.1. List of drugs to be considered during cardiac arrest

Feature	Drug to be considered	Route
Cardiac arrest	1 mg adrenaline (epinephrine) every 3–5 minutes	IV
Persistent VF/VT	300 mg amiodarone (once only)	IV
Asystole/bradycardia	3 mg atropine (once only)	IV
Opiate overdose	0.4–0.8 mg naloxone	IV
Magnesium toxicity	10 mg calcium gluconate	IV
Bupivicaine toxicity	intralipid infusion	IV

The cardiac arrest team leader should decide when a resuscitation attempt should be abandoned. This should be done in consultation with the rest of the team. They are also responsible for documenting the arrest and ensuring that staff and relatives are well supported after the arrest.

It is good practice to ensure someone remains with the relatives at all times during an arrest and keeps them informed as much as possible.

Recognition of heart rhythms

Resuscitation attempts should follow the predetermined evidenced based algorithms published by the Resuscitation Council UK.[1] The ALS algorithm (Figure 4.1) has two main pathways: those requiring direct current cardioversion ('shockable rhythms') and those in which this would be inappropriate ('non-shockable rhythms') (Box 4.2). The cardiac rhythm dictates which pathway to follow.

Box 4.2. Heart rhythms found during cardiac arrest

Shockable rhythms	Non-shockable rhythms
Ventricular fibrillation (VF)	Asystole
Pulseless ventricular tachycardia (VT)	Pulseless electrical activity (PEA)

Once cardiac arrest is confirmed, a defibrillator should be used to rapidly assess the cardiac rhythm of the woman. Self-adhesive pads are placed on the woman's chest and may be used for both cardiac monitoring and/or defibrillation. The ECG leads are colour coded and should be attached over bone with the red electrode to the right shoulder (Red to Right), the yellow electrode to the left shoulder (yeLLow to Left) and the green electrode below the pectoral muscles (green for spleen) (Figure 4.2). The defibrillator should be altered to read the ECG rhythm through lead two. Alternatively, the cardiac rhythm may be viewed through the self-adhesive defibrillator paddles attached to the woman's chest as illustrated in Figure 4.2.

During arrest, the heart rhythms seen will fit into one of the two categories: shockable or non-shockable (Table 4.2).

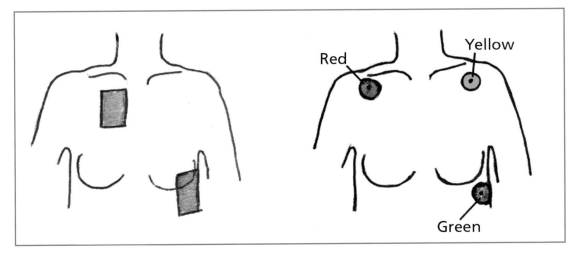

Figure 4.2. Defibrillation paddle and ECG electrode placement

Shockable rhythms

The majority of survivors from cardiac arrests come from the shockable rhythm category (VF and pulseless VT). A typical example of ventricular fibrillation is shown in Figure 4.3.

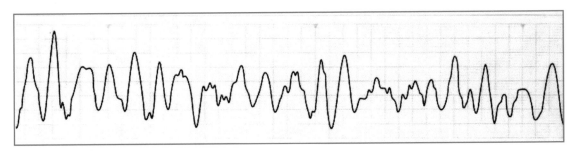

Figure 4.3. An example of ventricular fibrillation

Ventricular tachycardia is characterised by a broad complex regular tachycardia (Figure 4.4). VT can cause a profound loss of cardiac output and can suddenly deteriorate into VF. Pulseless VT is treated in the same way as VF.

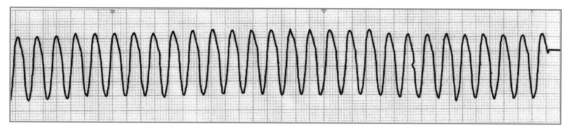

Figure 4.4. Ventricular tachycardia

Shockable cardiac rhythms need to be treated by defibrillation. This involves passing an electrical current across the heart to simultaneously depolarise a critical mass of the myocardium so that the natural pacemaking tissue of the heart can resume control. Attempted defibrillation is the single most important step in the treatment of VF/VT. The time between the onset of VF/VT and defibrillation is the main determinant of patient survival. Survival falls by 7–10% for each minute following collapse.

Most defibrillators now transmit a biphasic current, which has a higher efficiency so less energy is required to depolarise the heart. When using a biphasic defibrillator a current of 150–200 Joules (J) should be used for the first shock, and 150–360 J for subsequent shocks; for a monophasic defibrillator 360 J should be used for the first and subsequent shocks.

Know your machine: if unsure, shock at 200 J

Remember: only one shock per cycle is given for shockable rhythms; the shock is then immediately followed by 2 minutes of CPR at a ratio of 30 compressions to 2 ventilations (without checking for a rhythm or a pulse). After 2 minutes, the rhythm should be checked and a second shock delivered, if required. A pulse should only be checked if a non-shockable rhythm is seen.

Adrenaline (epinephrine) 1 mg IV should be given before alternate shocks (every 3–5 minutes), starting before third shock.

Most clinical areas now have automated external defibrillators (AEDs), which are able to analyse the cardiac rhythm and deliver appropriate shocks if indicated.

Non-shockable rhythms

Pulseless electrical activity (PEA) signifies the clinical absence of cardiac output (that is, no pulse) despite cardiac electrical activity, which may be normal (sinus rhythm or near normal). For example, in exsanguination, the heart's electrical activity may continue to show a normal sinus rhythm, as shown in Figure 4.5 but there is no circulating blood so a pulse is not present.

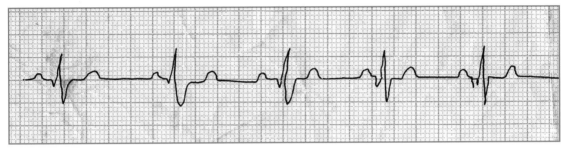

Figure 4.5. Normal sinus rhythm or electrical activity that can be found in pulseless electrical activity

Asystole is a slightly wandering flat line an example is shown in Figure 4.6. Sometimes very fine VF can look like asystole. If asystole is seen on a monitor, the gain (how vertically stretched the rhythm is) should be turned up to try and distinguish between the rhythms.

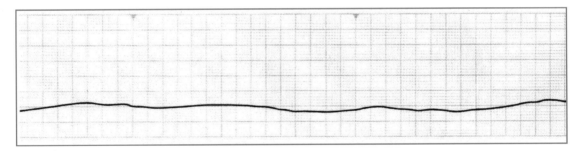

Figure 4.6. Asystole

> If there is any doubt about whether the rhythm is asystole or fine VF, **do not** attempt defibrillation; instead, continue chest compressions and ventilation 30:2.

A completely flat horizontal line indicates that the monitoring leads are not correctly attached rather than asystole, until proven otherwise. Adults in asystole have a very poor prognosis.

Adrenaline 1 mg IV should be given as soon as possible and then every 3–5 minutes. Atropine 3 mg IV can be given once for asystole or PEA with a heart rate of less than 60 beats/minute.

Potentially reversible causes

If the cardiac rhythm is not ventricular fibrillation or ventricular tachycardia, the outcome will be poor unless a potentially reversible cause can be found and treated. Potentially reversible causes of cardiac arrest can be remembered using four 'H's' and four 'T's'.

The four Hs

1. **Hypoxia** should be minimised by ensuring that the patient is adequately ventilated during the arrest. Basic life support followed by prompt intubation and ventilation using 100% oxygen should maximise oxygen delivery to the woman. She should be examined to check for chest rise and bilateral air entry during ventilation.

2. **Hypovolaemia** is most commonly caused by massive haemorrhage (such as abruption or postpartum haemorrhage). Intravenous fluids and blood products should be started promptly to restore the intravascular volume and urgent surgery to correct the cause of bleeding should be considered.

3. **Hypo/hyperkalaemia/metabolic**
   - **Hypoglycaemia** may occur in a diabetic mother. If the blood glucose measures below 3 mmol/l, give 50mls of 10% glucose solution IV.
   - **Hyperkalaemia** (high serum potassium) can develop secondary to renal failure.
   - **Hypermagnesaemia** (high serum magnesium) may result from treatment of pre-eclampsia with intravenous magnesium sulphate, especially with concurrent renal impairment.
   - **Hypocalcaemia** (low serum calcium) can result from overdose of calcium channel blocking drugs such as nifedipine.

   High serum levels of potassium or magnesium and low serum levels of calcium should be treated with 10 ml of 10% calcium gluconate IV.

4. **Hypothermia** is an unlikely cause of maternal arrest in hospital. Attempts should be made to keep patients warm in the periarrest situation by using warmed intravenous fluids and warming blankets if appropriate.

The four Ts

1. **Thromboemboli** are more common in pregnancy, owing to the procoagulant effect of pregnancy and the mechanical obstruction to venous return caused by the gravid uterus. Massive pulmonary embolus can cause sudden collapse and cardiac arrest. Treatment is difficult but thrombolysis, cardiopulmonary bypass or operative removal of the clot should be considered. Amniotic fluid emboli are also a cause of sudden collapse and cardiac arrest. Treatment remains supportive and care should be taken to correct clotting abnormalities as disseminated intravascular coagulopathy often results. Early liaison with haematology is essential.

2. **Tension pneumothorax** can cause collapse and subsequent PEA. A tension pneumothorax is most likely to occur during attempted central venous line insertion or trauma. Treatment involves acute decompression of the affected side by inserting a large intravenous cannula into the thoracic cavity in the second intercostal space at the midclavicular line, followed by chest drain insertion.

3. **Therapeutic** or **toxic** substances (for examples, inadvertent administration of lignocaine intravenously or opiate overdose) can cause arrest. Specific antidotes should be used; for example, for opiate overdose, naloxone 0.4–0.8 mg IV or for bupivicaine overdose, IV intralipid.

4. Cardiac **tamponade** is an uncommon cause of maternal arrest but should be considered in trauma, especially when there are penetrating chest injuries. Treatment involves relieving the tamponade by needle pericardiocentesis.

Drugs used during cardiac arrest

Adrenaline (epinephrine) 1mg should be given IV every 3–5 minutes during a cardiac arrest. Other drugs that may be considered are listed in Table 4.1.

All drugs should be flushed with at least 20 ml water for injections to ensure they enter the central circulation. The most common drugs required for a cardiac arrest are kept on the resuscitation trolley in prefilled syringes so that they can be quickly administered in an emergency. It is important that all staff are aware of the location of the emergency trolley and defibrillator within their own unit. It is also important that staff familiarise themselves with the use of the emergency equipment and drugs, as equipment may vary between locations.

References

1. Resuscitation Council (UK) [www.resus.org.uk].

2. European Resuscitation Council [www.erc.edu].

3. Goodwin AP, Pearce AJ. The human wedge: a manoeuvre to relieve aortocaval compression in resuscitation during late pregnancy. *Anaesthesia* 1992;47:433–4.

4. Marx G. Cardiopulmonary resuscitation of late pregnant women. *Anaesthesiology* 1982;56:156.

5. Oates S, Williams GL, Res GAD. Cardiopulmonary resuscitation in late pregnancy. *Br Med J* 1988;297:404.

6. Page-Rodriguez A, Gonzalez-Sanchez JA. Perimortem caesarean section of twin pregnancy: case report and review of the literature. *Acad Emerg Med* 1994;11:57–8.

7. Zakowski MI, Ramanathan S. CPR in pregnancy. *Curr Rev Clin Anesth* 1990;10:106.

Further reading

Advanced Life Support Working Group of the European Resuscitation Council. The 1998 European Resuscitation Council guidelines for adult advanced life support. *BMJ* 1998;316:1863–9.

American Heart Association in collaboration with the International Liaison Committee on Resuscitation. Guidelines for Cardiopulmonary Resuscitation and Emergency Cardiovascular Care – An International Consensus on Science. *Resuscitation* 2000;46:3–430.

Module 5
Intrapartum fetal monitoring

Key learning points

■ Recall the features of a normal, suspicious and pathological CTG.

■ Recall normal and abnormal fetal pH values.

■ Demonstrate ability to interpret the CTG, taking into account clinical circumstances and propose appropriate action.

■ Document details of opinion and management accurately, clearly and legibly.

Lessons learned from case discussions

■ When continuous EFM is recommended, the fetal heart should be auscultated simultaneously using a Pinard stethoscope at the start of the CTG, to confirm the fetal heart rate.

■ When continuous EFM is recommended during labour, a systematic assessment of the CTG based on the NICE algorithm should be documented at least hourly, including action to be taken.

■ When a pathological CTG is identified and delivery is expedited, EFM should be continued until delivery.

Introduction

Electronic fetal heart rate monitoring (EFM) was first introduced at Yale University.[1] In the UK, the clinical use of EFM began in the late 1960s.[2] At that time, it was not uncommon for babies to die in labour, apparently with few premonitory signs. When EFM was first introduced, the original aim was to prevent intrapartum fetal deaths. It was later assumed that EFM would allow earlier detection of hypoxia and that timely intervention would reduce cerebral palsy rates.

Meta-analysis of randomised controlled trials of EFM compared with intermittent auscultation have shown no difference in perinatal outcome but have shown an increase in operative delivery, particularly caesarean section, with EFM. However, the intervention rate was reduced when fetal blood sampling was used as an adjunct to EFM.[3,4]

It has been suggested that the lack of improvement in perinatal outcome, despite the use of EFM, could be due to the insufficient sample size of most randomised trials. Very large studies (35 000 women) would be required to determine the efficacy of EFM. The largest intrapartum fetal monitoring trial, the Dublin trial, found a reduction in neonatal seizures in the EFM arm but no difference in long term outcome.[5] However, the trial was not large enough to detect differences in the rates of cerebral palsy, as perinatal morbidity and mortality are extremely low. In addition, only about 10% of cerebral palsy cases are related to intrapartum events, as occult infection and/or inflammation are increasingly implicated.[6,7]

It is often forgotten that most randomised trials of EFM and intermittent auscultation have shown that neither method is particularly reliable and that there are important 'human' factors. Murphy et al.[8] found that, of 64 cases of significant birth asphyxia, abnormalities were missed in both continuously monitored and intermittent auscultation groups.

Inadequate skill in the interpretation of CTGs and failure to take appropriate action once abnormalities have been detected are key problems. This may have contributed to the failure of EFM to reduce perinatal mortality. These problems have been recurrent themes in many of the CESDI reports.[9–11] Grant highlighted that: 'for monitoring to be effective, it must be performed correctly, its results must then be interpreted satisfactorily; and this interpretation must provoke an appropriate response'.[3]

The West Midlands Perinatal Audit found that 70% of intrapartum deaths were considered to have avoidable factors, notably a lack of understanding in CTG interpretation.[12] Consequently, regular training and updates in CTG interpretation have been recommended by CESDI and this has now been implemented in the majority of maternity units in England and Wales.[11]

In 2001, the Royal College of Obstetricians and Gynaecologists produced an evidence-based guideline on fetal monitoring in labour, which has now been inherited by NICE.[13] The guideline not only aims to clarify when EFM is an appropriate method for monitoring the fetal heart in labour, but also standardises the classification of CTGs and provides guidance on actions to be taken when abnormalities are detected. There has been a further review of fetal monitoring in labour in the NICE *Intrapartum Care* guideline.[14]

Risk management

Both intrapartum death and the birth of a baby with severe brain damage are tragedies to the families concerned. The evidence linking brain injury to intrapartum care is inconsistent but it is a major source of litigation.[15,16] The basis of many claims includes:

- action taken too late
- intermittent auscultation was infrequent
- failure to call medical staff soon enough or often enough.[17]

If care is found to be suboptimal this is likely to be indefensible in court and claims can exceed £3 million. Adequate interpretation of CTGs is crucial to quality improvement and the reduction of medico-legal risk. In the UK, claims for damaged babies account for 80% of the NHS litigation bill.[18]

All practitioners involved in intrapartum care should ensure that they have the knowledge and skills to interpret CTGs and act appropriately, with the aim of providing high-quality, defensible care. The Clinical Negligence Scheme for Trusts (CNST) Maternity Standards mandate 6-monthly updates for all relevant staff.[18]

Physiology and pathophysiology

The healthy fetus is able to cope with the stresses of labour and adapts appropriately to meet the challenge. The evidence base supports the use of intermittent auscultation for 'low' risk mothers.

Fetal oxygen supply

In comparison with adults, the fetal partial pressure of oxygen is relatively low but the fetus has a remarkable margin of safety. The higher concentration of fetal haemoglobin and its greater affinity for oxygen means that oxygen saturation is high. The cardiac output of the fetus is also extremely efficient. Consequently, the fetal oxygen supply is usually greater than requirements.

Gas exchange is impaired during contractions, which means that oxygen levels fall and carbon dioxide (CO_2) levels rise. Between contractions the oxygen supply is restored and the accumulated CO_2 is excreted.

Conditions that impair gas exchange at the placenta, such as uterine hypercontractility, cord occlusion, maternal hypotension or abruption, will cause retention of CO_2, which lowers the pH of the fetal blood (a respiratory acidosis). This should be resolved when placental perfusion is restored. However, if gas exchange continues to be impeded, the fetus will rely on the following important defence mechanisms:

■ **Hormonal response**

A reduction in fetal oxygen supply is detected by chemoreceptors in the fetal aorta. This activates a hormonal response with an increase in catecholamines, vasopressin, adenine and adenosine levels. The levels of catecholamines in an asphyxiated infant exceed those of patients with phaeochromocytoma.[19]

■ **Preferential redistribution of blood flow**

There is a decrease in blood flow to less 'essential' organs such as the liver, spleen, gut, kidneys and skin. Blood supply to the 'priority' organs, brain, heart and adrenal glands, is increased. The heart needs to work harder during this time and myocardium blood flow can increase up to 500% in response to hypoxia. Oxygen requirements for the brain are not as great and fetal behaviour can adapt to reduce energy requirements.

■ **Glycogenolysis**

When the oxygen supply is no longer sufficient to meet the energy requirements of the fetus, glycogenolysis is activated by the hormonal response. This means that glucose is released from glycogen stores and is metabolised anaerobically (without oxygen) to maintain energy requirements. Release of adrenaline stimulates the activation of glycogenolysis.

During anaerobic metabolism, stores of glycogen in the heart, muscle and liver are broken down to provide energy. Lactic acid, a by-product of anaerobic metabolism, is initially buffered (neutralised) but will eventually cause the pH of the blood to fall further (metabolic acidosis). As the fetus continues to utilise glycogen stores, the acidosis becomes predominantly metabolic in origin and the pH decreases even further.

Clearly, conditions and events that affect the mother (pre-eclampsia, diabetes, antepartum haemorrhage) and/or placental function (too frequent or prolonged uterine contractions) and/or the baby's defence mechanisms (growth restriction, infection, chronic hypoxaemia and stress) may make the fetus less able to adapt and more vulnerable to hypoxia (Box 5.1).

Box 5.1. Factors that influence fetal oxygenation

Mother:

- Anaemia
- Analgesia/anaesthesia
- Dehydration
- Hypertension
- Hypotension
- Pyrexia

Uterus/placenta:

- Abruption
- Cord prolapse
- Impaired placental function
- Uterine hypercontractility

Fetus:

- Anaemia
- Fetal bleeding
- Infection
- Growth restriction

Compensatory responses and adaptation to hypoxia can only protect the fetus for a finite amount of time. When the defence mechanisms are blunted, depleted or overwhelmed, the risk of perinatal asphyxia (hypoxia, acidosis and tissue damage) is increased.

Standards and quality

The indications for offering women continuous EFM have been contemporaneously documented in the NICE *Intrapartum Care* guideline,[14] which should be implemented locally and available on every labour ward. The guideline recommends that risk factors should be recorded in the mother's notes as part of the admission assessment, together with appropriate action plans (Figure 5.1).[14]

Informed choice

The assessment of fetal wellbeing is only one aspect of intrapartum care. It is important that attention is given to an informed choice based on the available evidence. An information leaflet, *Monitoring your baby's heartbeat in labour: information for pregnant women* is available for download from the NICE website.[20]

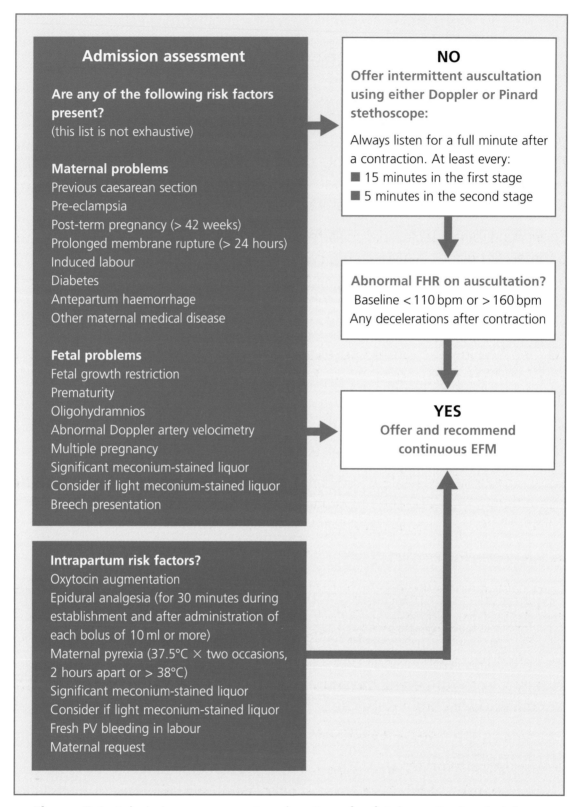

Admission assessment

Are any of the following risk factors present?
(this list is not exhaustive)

Maternal problems
Previous caesarean section
Pre-eclampsia
Post-term pregnancy (> 42 weeks)
Prolonged membrane rupture (> 24 hours)
Induced labour
Diabetes
Antepartum haemorrhage
Other maternal medical disease

Fetal problems
Fetal growth restriction
Prematurity
Oligohydramnios
Abnormal Doppler artery velocimetry
Multiple pregnancy
Significant meconium-stained liquor
Consider if light meconium-stained liquor
Breech presentation

Intrapartum risk factors?
Oxytocin augmentation
Epidural analgesia (for 30 minutes during establishment and after administration of each bolus of 10 ml or more)
Maternal pyrexia (37.5°C × two occasions, 2 hours apart or > 38°C)
Significant meconium-stained liquor
Consider if light meconium-stained liquor
Fresh PV bleeding in labour
Maternal request

NO
Offer intermittent auscultation using either Doppler or Pinard stethoscope:

Always listen for a full minute after a contraction. At least every:
■ 15 minutes in the first stage
■ 5 minutes in the second stage

Abnormal FHR on auscultation?
Baseline < 110 bpm or > 160 bpm
Any decelerations after contraction

YES
Offer and recommend continuous EFM

Figure 5.1. Admission assessment and options for fetal monitoring in labour (based on NICE Guidelines 2001 & 2007)[13,14]

Technical considerations

It is best to auscultate the fetal heart using a Pinard stethoscope before commencing EFM. In addition, the maternal pulse should be palpated regularly with any form of fetal monitoring, to differentiate between maternal and fetal heart rates. On rare occasions, when EFM is used, it is possible to generate a signal from a large pulsating maternal vessel. Also, the ultrasound may falsely double the rate of the maternal pulse if there is sufficient extended separation between valve movements, generating a rate that would be within the normal range of the fetal heart.

There have been occasional reports of unexpected macerated stillbirths with apparently normal intrapartum CTGs, even with direct fetal scalp clip application.[21,22] It is therefore important that, if fetal death is suspected despite the presence of an apparently recordable fetal heart rate, fetal viability should be confirmed with real-time ultrasound assessment.

All members of staff should be aware of the technical limitations of EFM and should always read the manufacturer's instructions for each particular monitor.

Standards for intermittent auscultation

For a mother who is healthy and has an uncomplicated pregnancy, intermittent auscultation should be offered and recommended in labour using either a Doppler ultrasound or a Pinard stethoscope, to monitor fetal wellbeing.

In the active stages of labour:

■ First stage of labour: intermittent auscultation should occur at least every 15 minutes, after a contraction, and for a minimum of 60 seconds.

■ Second stage of labour: intermittent auscultation should occur every 5 minutes, after a contraction, and for a minimum of 60 seconds.

■ Any intrapartum events that may affect the fetal heart rate should be noted contemporaneously in the maternal notes, signed and the time noted.

Continuous EFM should be offered and recommended when:

■ a baseline of less than 110 beats/minute or greater than 160 beats/minute is heard during intermittent auscultation

■ any decelerations are suspected after a contraction

■ any intrapartum risk factors develop (see Figure 5.1).

The current evidence base does not support the use of the admission CTG in low-risk pregnancies and is therefore not recommended.

Standards for electronic fetal monitoring

EFM should not be used as a tool of convenience in place of skilled midwives. The unselected use of continuous EFM contributes to unnecessary intervention.

- The date and time clocks on the machine should be correct and paper speed set to 1cm/minute.

- CTGs should be labelled with the mother's name and hospital number and dated.

- Any intrapartum events that may affect the fetal heart rate should be noted contemporaneously on the CTG, signed and dated (such as vaginal examinations, fetal blood sampling, epidural insertion and top-ups).

- If external monitoring is not of sufficient quality for interpretation of the CTG, a fetal scalp electrode should be applied where possible.

- Any consultations should be documented in the case notes and on the CTG, together with the date, time and signature.

- Following the birth, the caregiver should sign and note the date, time and mode of delivery on the CTG.

- The CTG should be stored securely with the maternal notes.

Features of the CTG and terminology

Most clinicians would have no difficulty in recognising the features of a normal CTG, as shown in Figure 5.2. However, it is important to remember that a suspicious or pathological CTG does not necessarily mean the fetus is hypoxic (insufficient oxygen to meet requirements). In fact, often this is not the case, as illustrated in Figure 5.3. When the CTG is normal, we can be fairly confident that the fetus will be normoxic, so the sensitivity of the CTG is high. However, when the CTG is pathological or suspicious, only about 50% of fetuses will show some degree of hypoxia, so its specificity is low.

In addition, there is no reliable way to determine fetal reserves or, often, the nature or severity of the event. The growth-restricted fetus may have a blunted response owing to chronic stress and inadequate glycogen stores. Acute catastrophic events may quickly overwhelm the defence mechanism of even a healthy baby. The CTG must thus always be interpreted in the context of the antepartum and intrapartum events.

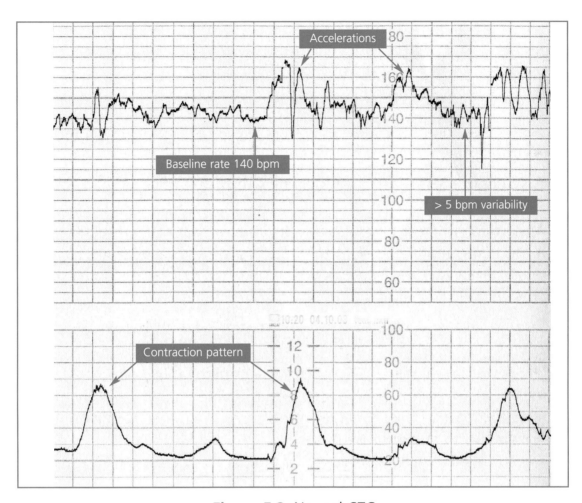

Figure 5.2. Normal CTG

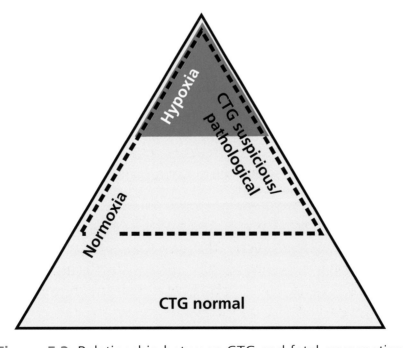

Figure 5.3. Relationship between CTG and fetal oxygenation

Clearly, it is important that communication between carers should convey the clinical context using consistent terminology to describe the features of the CTG, the level of concern and the urgency of the situation.

There are four main features that should be systematically examined to assist with the interpretation of the CTG:

- baseline rate
- baseline variability
- accelerations
- decelerations.

These features, in conjunction with the contraction pattern and the clinical circumstances, should all be considered when deciding the action to be taken.

Baseline fetal heart rate

Baseline fetal heart rate is the level of the fetal heart rate when it is stable, excluding accelerations and decelerations. It is determined over a time period of 5 or 10 minutes and expressed in beats/minute (see Figure 5.2). The ranges and descriptive terms are shown in Table 5.1.

Table 5.1. Baseline ranges

Level	Rate (beats/minute)
Reassuring	
Normal Baseline	110–160
Non-reassuring	
Moderate bradycardia	100–109
Moderate tachycardia[a]	161–180
Abnormal	
Abnormal bradycardia	< 100
Abnormal tachycardia	> 180

[a] A tachycardia of 161–180 beats/minute (bpm), where accelerations are present and no other adverse features appear, should NOT be regarded as suspicious. However, an increase in the baseline rate, even within the normal range, with other non-reassuring or abnormal features should increase concern[14]

Baseline variability

Baseline variability is the minor fluctuation in baseline fetal heart rate occurring at three to five cycles/minute (see Figure 5.2).

Normal baseline variability:	Greater or equal to 5 beats/minute between contractions for up to 40 minutes.
Non-reassuring baseline variability:	Less than 5 beats/minute for 40 minutes or more but less than 90 minutes.
Abnormal baseline variability:	Less than 5 beats/minute for 90 minutes or more.

Note that, if repeated accelerations are present with reduced variability, the CTG should be regarded as reassuring.[14]

Accelerations

Accelerations are an abrupt transient increase in the fetal heart rate of 15 beats/minute or more, lasting 15 seconds or more (Figure 5.2). The absence of accelerations with an otherwise normal CTG is of uncertain significance.

Decelerations

Decelerations are a transient slowing of the fetal heart rate below the baseline level of 15 beats/minutes or more for a period of 15 seconds or more.

Early decelerations:	Uniform, repetitive, periodic slowing of the fetal heart rate with onset early in the contraction and return to baseline at the end of the contraction. The lowest point of the deceleration will coincide with the highest point of the contraction. Early decelerations are usually associated with head compression and hence tend to occur late in the first stage or during the second stage of labour. True uniform early decelerations are rare and benign and are therefore not significant and not associated with fetal hypoxia.
Late decelerations:	Uniform, repetitive, periodic slowing of the fetal heart rate with onset mid- to end of the contraction and lowest point more than 20 seconds after the peak of the contraction, always ending after the contraction. In the presence of a non-accelerative trace with

baseline variability less than 5 beats/minute, the definition would include decelerations less than 15 beats/minute. Late decelerations, if present for more than 30 minutes are always indicative of fetal hypoxia and further action is indicated (Figure 5.4).[14]

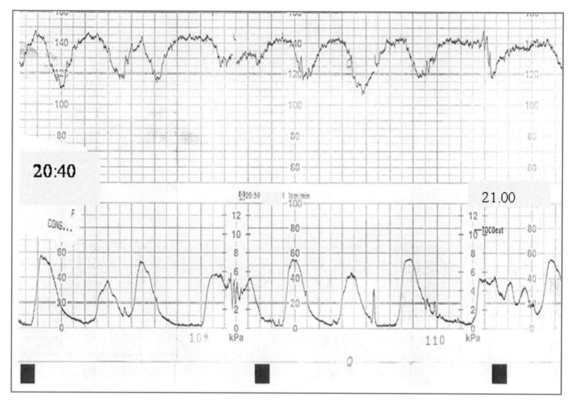

Figure 5.4. Late decelerations

Variable decelerations: These are the most common form of deceleration occurring during labour. A variable, intermittent periodic slowing of the fetal heart rate, with rapid onset and recovery. Time relationships with contraction cycle are variable and they occur in isolation. Sometimes they resemble other types of deceleration patterns in timing and shape. They are often caused by compression of the umbilical cord, and can be typical or atypical (Figure 5.5). Typical variable decelerations are an autonomic nervous system response to cord compression and are indicative of the fetus coping well. However, the fetus may become tired over time and, if they occur with over 50% of contractions for more than 90 minutes, this should be regarded as non-

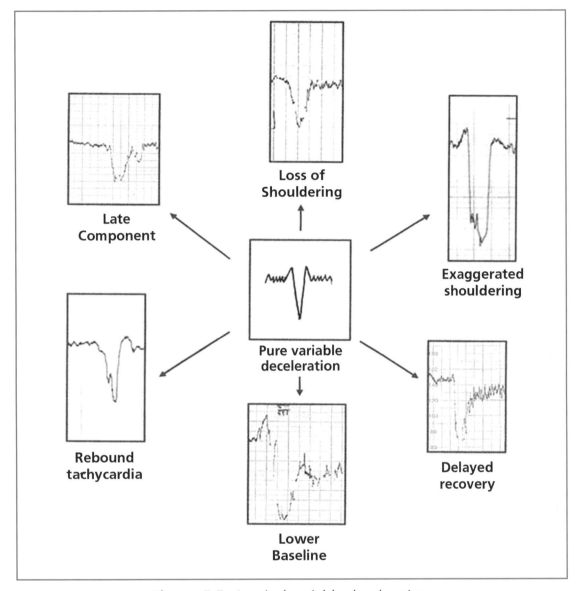

Figure 5.5. Atypical variable decelerations

reassuring, particularly if there is any degree of fetal compromise such as intrauterine growth restriction.[14] Atypical variable decelerations may subsequently develop indicating that the fetus is now less able to cope with the cord compression.

Atypical variable decelerations: Variable decelerations with any of the following components (Figure 5.5):

- loss of primary or secondary rise in baseline rate
- slow return to baseline FHR after the end of the contraction

- prolonged secondary rise in baseline rate
- a biphasic deceleration
- loss of variability during deceleration
- continuation of baseline rate at lower level.

If atypical variable decelerations occur with more than 50% of contractions for over 30 minutes, they should be defined as abnormal and the CTG is therefore pathological, indicating that further action is required.[14]

Prolonged deceleration: An abrupt decrease in the fetal heart rate to levels below the baseline that lasts for at least 60–90 seconds. If a fetal bradycardia occurs for more than 3 minutes, plans should be made to urgently expedite delivery. A 'category 1 birth' should be declared and the woman should be transferred to theatre immediately. If the fetal heart recovers within 9 minutes, the decision for immediate delivery should be reconsidered, if reasonable, and in consultation with the woman.

Sinusoidal pattern: A regular oscillation of the baseline long-term variability resembling a sine wave. This smooth, undulating pattern, lasting at least 10 minutes, has a relatively fixed period of 3–5 cycles/minute and an amplitude of 5–15 beats/minute above and below the baseline. Baseline variability is absent. A true sinusoidal pattern is an abnormal feature and is associated with high rates of fetal morbidity and mortality (Figure 5.6).[23]

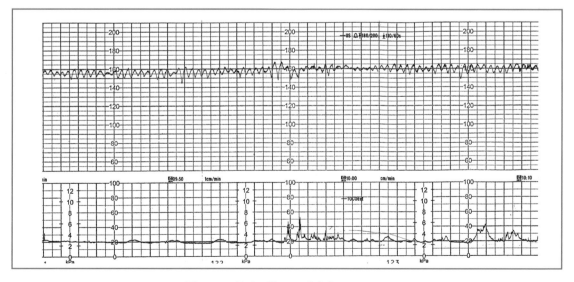

Figure 5.6. Sinusoidal pattern

Contraction
pattern:
Always remember to look at the 'bottom line'. Take notice of the duration of contractions and the interval between contractions. Frequent, low amplitude contractions, in association with an abnormal CTG, is suggestive of placental abruption.

Interpretation of the CTG

There are four main features that should be observed when interpreting a CTG. A trace may be classified as normal, suspicious or pathological, depending on the presence of any non-reassuring or abnormal features. The clinical circumstances should always be considered when deciding actions to be taken if a CTG is suspicious or pathological. A CTG pro forma, based on the NICE *Intrapartum Care* guideline, can be used to document the four main features and classification of the CTG.[14] This information, together with the clinical findings and any subsequent action to be taken, can also be documented on the pro forma (Figure 5.7).

Digital stimulation of the fetal scalp by the healthcare professional during a vaginal examination should be considered as an adjunct to continuous EFM.[14]

Suspicious CTG

A CTG with one non-reassuring feature is classified as suspicious. Figure 5.8 shows the NICE guidelines suggested actions when the CTG is suspicious.

Pathological CTG and fetal blood sampling

A CTG with two or more non-reassuring features **or** one or more abnormal features is classified as pathological. Units that employ EFM should have ready access to fetal blood sampling facilities. When delivery is contemplated because of a pathological CTG and acidosis is suspected, fetal blood sampling is recommended in the absence of technical difficulties or contraindications.

Contraindications include:

■ maternal infection (for example HIV, hepatitis viruses and herpes simplex virus)

■ fetal bleeding disorders (for example haemophilia)

■ prematurity (less than 34 weeks).

North Bristol NHS Trust	Reassuring	Non-reassuring	Abnormal	
Baseline rate	110–160 bpm	– 100–109 bpm – 161–180 bpm	– Less than 100 bpm – Over 180 bpm – Sinusoidal pattern for 10 minutes or more	Comments:
Variability	5 bpm or more	Less than 5 bpm for 40 – 90 mins (in the absence of accelerations)	Less than 5 bpm for 90 minutes (in the absence of accelerations)	Comments:
Accelerations	Present	Comments:		
Decelerations	None	– Typical variable decelerations with over 50% of contractions for over 90 minutes – Single prolonged deceleration up to 3 minutes	– Atypical variable decelerations with over 50% of contractions for over 30 minutes – Late decelerations for over 30 minutes – Single prolonged deceleration more than 3 minutes	Comments:
Opinion	Normal CTG (All four features reassuring)	Suspicious CTG (One non-reassuring feature)	Pathological CTG (two or more non-reassuring or one or more abnormal features)	

Dilatation (cm)	Cont's	:10	Liquor colour	Mat pulse
Action				

Date .... Time............... Signature....................... Status.................

Figure 5.7. A pro forma for classification of CGT and subsequent action

Suspicious CTG

Ensure adequate quality recording of both fetal heart rate and contraction pattern

Inadequate quality CTG?

Check maternal pulse

Poor contact from external transducer?

- check position of transducer
- consider applying fetal scalp electrode (FSE)

FSE not working?

- Check position of electrode
- Confirm fetal heart with Pinard stethoscope and/or ultrasound

Uterine hypercontractility?

Is the mother receiving oxytocin?

- Reduce/stop infusion

Has the mother recently received vaginal prostaglandins?

- Consider tocolysis with subcutaneous terbutaline 0.25 mg

Maternal tachycardia/pyrexia

Is there a maternal infection?

- Check temperature. If 37.5°C on two occasions, 2 hours apart or 38.0°C or higher, consider screening and treatment

Is mother dehydrated?

- Check blood pressure and give 500 ml crystalloid (IV) if appropriate

Is mother receiving tocolytic infusion?

- If maternal pulse > 140 bpm, reduce infusion

Other maternal factors

What is the mother's position?

- Encourage mother to adopt left-lateral position

Consider:

- Is mother hypotensive?
- Has a vaginal examination just been performed?
- Has mother been vomiting or had a vasovagal episode?
- Has mother just had epidural sited?

Check blood pressure and give 500 ml crystalloid (IV) if appropriate

If CTG remains suspicious, continue to observe for further non-reassuring or abnormal features and always consider in context with clinical circumstances.

If CTG becomes pathological, see actions for pathological CTG

Figure 5.8. Suggested actions if CTG suspicious

Pathological CTG

Fetal blood sampling (FBS) possible and/or appropriate?
Encourage mother to adopt left lateral position. Check blood pressure and give 500 ml crystalloid (IV) if appropriate.

FBS result (pH)	Recommended action
Normal **7.25 or above**	– FBS should be repeated in 1 hour if FHR abnormality persists or sooner if there are further abnormalities – If result remains stable after second test, a third/further sample may be deferred unless there are further abnormalities of the CTG
Borderline **7.21 – 7.24**	– Repeat FBS within 30 minutes if the FHR remains pathological or sooner if there are further abnormalities. (consideration should be given to the time taken to perform FBS when planning repeat samples) – If a third sample is indicated, a consultant obstetric opinion should be sought
Abnormal **7.20 or less**	– Consultant obstetric advice should be sought – Urgent delivery within 30 minutes

All FBS results should be interpreted taking into account the previous pH measurement, the rate of progress in labour and the clinical features of mother and fetus.

Fetal blood sampling not possible/inappropriate?
– Encourage mother to adopt left lateral position. Check blood pressure and give 500 ml crystalloid (IV) if appropriate.

EXPEDITE DELIVERY:
– The urgency and mode of delivery should take into account the severity of the fetal heart rate and the clinical circumstances.
– The accepted standard is that delivery should be accomplished within 30 minutes.

Figure 5.9. Suggested actions if CTG pathological

Fetal blood sampling should be undertaken with the mother in the left-lateral position. Figure 5.9 shows suggested actions if the CTG is pathological.[14]

If fetal blood sampling proves to be technically difficult and a sample cannot be obtained, then the baby should be delivered as soon as possible, based on the clinical circumstances of the mother, baby and the CTG.

Where there is clear evidence of acute fetal compromise (for example, a prolonged deceleration for longer than 3 minutes) fetal blood sampling should not be undertaken and the baby should be delivered urgently. Ideally, delivery should be accomplished within 30 minutes, taking into account the severity of the situation.

If there is an abnormal fetal heart rate pattern and uterine hypercontractility, which is not secondary to the use of an oxytocin infusion, tocolysis should be considered. The suggested regimen is subcutaneous terbutaline 0.25 mg.[14] Its use may also be considered to reduce uterine activity and aid in-utero resuscitation when preparing for a category 1 delivery. If terbutaline is used, anticipate the possibility of uterine atony post delivery and treat accordingly.

Adverse effects of terbutaline include maternal tachycardia (palpitations) and, hence, fetal tachycardia may occur. Raised blood pressure, tremor, nausea, nervousness and dizziness may also occur.

Continuous EFM in the presence of oxytocin

If the fetal heart rate is normal, an oxytocin infusion may be increased until the woman is experiencing four or five contractions every 10 minutes. The infusion rate should be reduced if contractions occur more frequently than five contractions in 10 minutes.

If the fetal heart rate trace is classified as suspicious when an oxytocin infusion is in progress, a review by an experienced obstetrician should be requested. Once reviewed, the obstetrician may recommend that the oxytocin continues to be increased but only to a dose which achieves four to five contractions in 10 minutes.[14]

If the fetal heart rate trace is classified as pathological, the oxytocin infusion should be stopped and a full assessment of the fetal condition should be undertaken by an experienced obstetrician before the oxytocin is recommenced.

The prolonged use of maternal facial oxygen therapy may be harmful to the fetus and should therefore be avoided. There is also currently no evidence evaluating the benefits or risks associated with the short-term use of maternal facial oxygen therapy in cases of suspected fetal compromise. However, the anaesthetist may request facial oxygen to be administered purely for maternal preoxygenation before an operative procedure.

Newborn assessment

The Apgar score, need for intubation and abnormal behaviour are important components of the assessment of the newborn baby. However, they are subjective, provide incomplete information and are not by themselves indicative of asphyxia. In the perinatal period, asphyxia is defined as the combination of hypoxia and acidosis with impaired organ function.[24] Thus, both clinical and biochemical information are required to differentiate between an asphyxiated infant and one that is depressed for other reasons (infection, congenital abnormalities or maternal analgesia). Paired samples from the umbilical artery and umbilical vein should be collected in order to provide an objective outcome measure. The RCOG recommends that paired samples should be obtained as a minimum when:

- emergency caesarean section is performed
- instrumental vaginal delivery is performed
- fetal blood sampling has been performed in labour
- the baby's condition is poor at birth, with an Apgar score at 5 minutes of 6 or less.

The umbilical cord acid-base status at time of birth can be important for medico-legal reasons and for risk management strategies.[25] Clamped cord segments or blood stored in syringes can be left at room temperature for up to 60 minutes without significant changes in pH or CO_2.[26,27]

Pre-course electronic fetal monitoring CTG workbook

A pre-course CTG workbook with case examples will be provided by your course tutor. Participants should complete the workbook before the course and should be ready to discuss the cases on the day of the course. The cases will be reviewed and discussed in small group sessions. The workbooks will not be scored or marked in any way.

References

1. Hon EH. The electronic evaluation of the fetal heart rate. *Am J Obstet Gynecol* 1958;75:1215.

2. Beard RW, Filshie GM, Knight CA, Roberts GM. The significance of the changes in the continuous fetal heart rate in the first stage of labour. *J Obstet Gynaecol Br Commonw* 1971;78:865–81.

3. Grant A. Monitoring the fetus during labour. In: Chalmers I, Enkin M, Keirse MC, editors. *Effective Care in Pregnancy and Childbirth*. Oxford: Oxford University Press; 1989. p. 846–82.

4. Thaker SB, Stroup DF, Chang M. Continuous electronic heart rate monitoring for fetal assessment during labor. *Cochrane Database Syst Rev* 2001;(2):CD000063.

5. MacDonald D, Grant A, Sheridan-Pereira M, Boylan P, Chalmers I. The Dublin randomised controlled trial of intrapartum fetal heart rate monitoring. *Am J Obstet Gynecol* 1985;152:524–39.

6. Nelson KB. What proportion of cerebral palsy is related to birth asphyxia? *J Pediatr* 1988;112:572–4.

7. Nelson KB, Willoughby RE. Infection, inflammation, and the risk of cerebral palsy. *Curr Opin Neurol* 2000;13:133–9.

8. Murphy KW, Johnson P, Moorcraft J, Pattison R, Russel V, Turnbull A. Birth asphyxia and the intrapartum cardiotocograph. *Br J Obstet Gynaecol* 1990;97:470–9.

9. Confidential Enquiry into Stillbirths and Deaths in Infancy. *4th Annual Report*. London: Maternal and Child Health Research Consortium1997.

10. Confidential Enquiry into Stillbirths and Deaths in Infancy. *5th Annual Report*. London: Maternal and Child Health Research Consortium; 1998.

11. Confidential Enquiry into Stillbirths and Deaths in Infancy. *7th Annual Report*. London: Maternal and Child Health Research Consortium; 2001.

12. West Midlands Perinatal Audit. Stillbirth and Neonatal Death 1991–1994. Report of National, Regional, District and Unit Mortality Rates. Keele: West Midlands Perinatal Audit; 1996.

13. Royal College of Obstetricians and Gynaecologists. *Electronic Fetal Monitoring. National Evidence-based Clinical Guideline*. London: RCOG Press; 2001.

14. National Collaborating Centre for Women's and Children's Health. *Intrapartum Care: care of healthy women and their babies during childbirth*. NICE Clinical guideline 55. London: RCOG Press; 2007.

15. Clements RV, Simanowitz A. Cerebral palsy: the international consensus statement. *Clinical Risk* 2000;6:135–6.

16. Pickering J. Legal comment on the international consensus statement on causation of cerebral palsy. *Clinical Risk* 2000;6:143–4.

17. Symonds EM. Litigation and birth related injuries. In: Chamberlain G, editor. *How to Avoid Medico-legal Problems in Obstetrics and Gynaecolog*y. London: Chameleon Press; 1991.

18. Clinical Negligence Scheme for Trusts. *Clinical Risk Management Standards For Maternity Services*. London: NHS Litigation Authority Clinical Negligence Scheme for Trusts; 2002.

19. Lagercrantz H, Bistoletti P. Catecholamine release in the newborn infant at birth. *Pediatr Res* 1977;11:889–93.

20. National Institute for Health and Clinical Excellence. *Monitoring Your Baby's Heartbeat in Labour: information for pregnant women*. London: NICE; 2001 [www.nice.org.uk/nicemedia/pdf/efmpatleafenglish.pdf].

21. Herbert WN, Stuart NN, Butler LS. (Electronic fetal heart rate monitoring with intrauterine fetal demise. *J Obstet Gynecol Neonatal Nurs* 1987;16:249–52.

22. Maeder HP, Lippert TH. Misinterpretation of heart rate recordings in fetal death *Eur J Obstet Gynecol* 1972;6:167–70.

23. Schneider EP, Tropper PJ. The variable deceleration, prolonged deceleration, and sinusoidal fetal heart rate. *Clin Obstet Gynecol* 1986;29:64–72.

24. Greene KR, Rosen KG. Intrapartum asphyxia. In: Levene MI, Lilford R, editors. *Fetal and Neonatal Neurology and Neurosurgery*. 2nd ed. Edinburgh: Churchill Livingstone; 1995. p. 389–404.

25. MacLennan A. A template for defining a causal relation between acute intrapartum events and cerebral palsy: international consensus statement. *BMJ* 1999;319:1054–5.

26. Duerbeck NB, Chaffin DG, Seeds JW. A practical approach to umbilical artery pH and blood gas determinations. *Obstet Gynecol* 1992;79:959–62.

27. Sykes GS, Molloy PM. Effects of delays in collection or analysis on the results of umbilical cord blood measurements. *Br J Obstet Gynaecol* 1984;91:989–92.

Module 6
Major obstetric haemorrhage

Key learning points

- To understand the main risk factors and causes of major obstetric haemorrhage.
- To emphasise the importance of early fluid resuscitation.
- To be familiar with the immediate management and treatment of postpartum haemorrhage (PPH) including bimanual uterine compression.
- Recall the drug doses and routes of administration for the treatment of uterine atony.
- To outline mechanical manoeuvres required to control torrential bleeding.
- To communicate effectively with the woman and the team.
- Document details of management accurately, clearly and legibly.

Common difficulties observed in training drills

- Delay in recognition of the problem, such as significant tachycardia but not initially hypotensive.
- Not stating the problem clearly to all who attend emergency.
- Delay in commencing resuscitation fluids.
- Underestimation of blood loss and delay in recognising need for transfer to theatre.
- Unsure of location of O-negative blood.

Introduction

Massive obstetric haemorrhage from abruption, placenta praevia and postpartum haemorrhage (PPH) is one of the main causes of maternal mortality worldwide, accounting for 11% of all maternal deaths. In the UK, the risk of a pregnant woman dying from haemorrhage is very small, with a mortality rate of 6.6/million maternities.[1] However, of the women that died in the most recent triennium (2003–05), over 50% received suboptimal care. In particular, there were concerns with the management of women with placenta percreta, a condition that is likely to become more prevalent, given its association with previous caesarean section scars. There were also failures identified in the recognition of signs and symptoms of intra-abdominal bleeding, particularly after caesarean section. Lastly, there were also deficiencies in the management of uterine atony, with a reluctance to use ergometrine and Syntocinon® (Alliance) as the drugs of first choice.[1]

Definition of postpartum haemorrhage

Traditionally, the definition of primary PPH is a blood loss of 500 ml or more within the first 24 hours after delivery (secondary PPH being a blood loss of 500 ml or more after 24 hours and up until 6 weeks postpartum). Most healthy women can cope with this amount of blood loss without problems.

In the UK, major PPH, a blood loss in excess of 1000 ml, occurs after 1.3% of deliveries.[3] Clinical signs include a disturbance of vital signs, with a pulse rate over 120 beats/minute and a systolic blood pressure of less than 100 mmHg. In obstetrics, a blood loss of over 1500 ml represents around 25% of the blood volume and is a potentially life-threatening complication.[4] Long-term morbidity includes renal impairment, Sheehan syndrome and blood borne transfusion infections.

The management of a major obstetric haemorrhage is broadly the same whatever the cause.

Risk factors for major postpartum haemorrhage

The main prelabour and intrapartum risk factors for PPH are listed in Box 6.1. Where there has been a previous PPH, the risk of recurrence is increased to about 8–10%. Other factors include primiparous women and maternal obesity. In the most recent maternal mortality report, 43% of women that died from PPH had a body mass index (BMI) of greater than 30.[1] Maternal age is also relevant, as older women may be less able to withstand the effects of severe blood loss.[5] Previous caesarean section is a risk factor for PPH, in particular because of its association with placenta praevia and placenta percreta or accreta. The risk of PPH is further increased with the number of previous caesarean sections.[1] Operative delivery, especially emergency caesarean section, substantially increases the risk of PPH.

Box 6.1. Risk factors for postpartum haemorrhage

Prelabour

- Placental abruption
- Placenta praevia
- Previous caesarean section
- Overdistension of uterus (e.g. multiple pregnancy, polyhydramnios, macrosomia)
- Grand multiparity (parity of 4 or more)
- Pre-eclampsia
- Previous retained placenta or postpartum haemorrhage
- Maternal Hb below 8.5 g/dl at start of labour
- Body mass index > 35 kg/m^2
- Maternal age (35 years or older)
- Existing uterine abnormalities
- Placenta accreta or percreta

Intrapartum

- Induction of labour
- Prolonged first, second or third stage of labour
- Oxytocin use in labour
- Precipitate labour
- Operative vaginal birth
- Caesarean section, particularly in the second stage of labour

---

Haemorrhagic disorders

Mothers with haemorrhagic disorders such as haemophilia require specialist care throughout pregnancy. There should be clear individualised care plans for labour documented in the woman's notes and experienced staff should provide intrapartum care.

Anaemia

Mothers who are anaemic are less able to tolerate blood loss of even apparently small amounts. Important aspects of antenatal care include antenatal screening of haemoglobin levels and treatment of anaemia.

Prevention of postpartum haemorrhage

There is a strong evidence base to support routine active management of the third stage of labour.[6,7] The use of intramuscular Syntometrine® (Alliance) reduces the risk of PPH by 60%. However, there is a five-fold increase in the incidence of nausea and vomiting. There is also an increase in the incidence of postpartum hypertension. Syntocinon® (Alliance) alone, given intramuscularly at a dose of 10 iu (or 5 iu if given intravenously), is slightly less effective at reducing initial blood loss, but is preferable in the presence of maternal hypertension or if the maternal blood pressure is not known before delivery.[1]

The likelihood of uterine atony should be anticipated in clinical situations such as prolonged labour or second stage caesarean section. Intramuscular Syntometrine (if appropriate) or slow intravenous Syntocinon should be given after delivery of the baby, followed by an infusion of Syntocinon 40 units in 500 ml 0.9% saline given intravenously (125 ml/hour) over the next 2–4 hours.[1]

The latest Confidential Enquiry recommends that women who have had a previous caesarean section should have their placental site determined and, if there is any doubt, magnetic resonance imaging (MRI) can be used along with ultrasound scanning to determine whether the placenta is accreta or percreta. If either is confirmed then forward planning in the antenatal period and the involvement of a large multidisciplinary team at delivery may prevent or reduce the risk of haemorrhage.[1]

Pathophysiology

The normal adult blood volume is approximately 70 ml/kg, which amounts to a total blood volume of about 5 litres. The healthy pregnant woman has a total blood volume of 6–7 litres in late pregnancy. This enhanced blood volume, in conjunction with increased levels of blood coagulation factors, such as fibrinogen and clotting factors VII, VIII and X, provides physiological protection against haemorrhage.

As mentioned previously, the traditional definition of primary PPH is a blood loss of 500 ml or more within the first 24 hours but this is now of little clinical relevance. Most healthy pregnant women cope with such loss without any problems. Blood loss can be difficult to estimate and bleeding can be concealed within the uterus, broad ligament or the uterine cavity. The normal blood loss at a vaginal delivery or at a caesarean section induces little or no change in pulse or blood pressure. Table 6.1 summarises the clinical features of shock in pregnancy related to the volume of blood loss.

Table 6.1. Clinical features of shock in pregnancy related to blood loss

Blood loss (ml)	Clinical features	Level of shock
500–1000	Normal blood pressure Tachycardia Palpitations, dizziness	Compensated
1000–1500	Hypotension systolic 90–80 mmHg Tachycardia Tachypnoea (21–30 breaths/minute) Pallor, sweating Weakness, faintness, thirst	Mild
1500–2000	Hypotension 80–60 mmHg Rapid, weak pulse > 110 beats/minute Tachypnoea (> 30 breaths/minute) Pallor, cold clammy skin Poor urinary output < 30 ml/hour Restlessness, anxiety, confusion.	Moderate
2000–3000	Severe hypotension < 50 mmHg Pallor, cold clammy skin, peripheral cyanosis Air hunger Anuria Confusion or unconsciousness, collapse	Severe

Causes of postpartum haemorrhage

Major PPH usually occurs within the first hour after delivery. The most common cause is an atonic uterus (70–90%), with or without retained placental tissue. Genital tract trauma is also common. Coagulation defects are less common. Table 6.2 lists some of the presenting features, which may be accompanied by signs and symptoms of shock listed in Table 6.1. It is important to remember that bleeding may also be concealed.

Table 6.2. Presenting features and causes of postpartum haemorrhage

Presenting features	Condition of uterus	Possible cause
Vaginal bleeding, placenta complete	Soft	Uterine atony
Vaginal bleeding, placenta incomplete	Soft or contracted	Retained placental tissue
Vaginal bleeding, placenta complete	Well contracted	Vaginal/cervical/perineal trauma
Mild or severe abdominal pain and symptoms of shock, often without vaginal bleeding	Seen at vulva/ not palpable abdominally	Inverted uterus
Vaginal bleeding, severe abdominal pain, shoulder tip pain	Tender/extremely painful on palpation	Ruptured uterus
Continual bleeding, oozing from wound sites	Soft or contracted	Coagulopathy

Rupture of the uterus usually occurs before or at the time of delivery but the diagnosis may not be made until after delivery.

A morbid adherence of the placenta to the myometrium (placenta percreta or accreta) is usually diagnosed when massive haemorrhage occurs following unsuccessful attempts to separate and remove the placenta. Profuse bleeding from a morbidly adherent placenta was responsible for 20% of deaths from PPH in the latest triennial maternal mortality report.[1] In addition, a case–control study of peripartum hysterectomy carried out by the United Kingdom Obstetric Surveillance System (UKOSS) reported that of the women requiring peripartum hysterectomy because of haemorrhage, 38% had a morbidly adherent placenta.[8,9]

Mothers with inherited haemorrhagic disorders, such as haemophilia and Von Willebrand's disease, are at risk of PPH. These mothers require specialist care. Hypertensive disorders of pregnancy such as HELLP syndrome (haemolysis, elevated liver enzymes, low platelets) also make the mother vulnerable to bleeding.

Coagulopathies may develop as a consequence of severe blood loss. In disseminated intravascular coagulation (DIC), blood is exposed to excessive amounts of pro-clotting factors including thromboplastin. Coagulation factors are consumed and the fibrinolytic system is activated. Control of coagulation balance and fibrinolysis is disrupted and may increasingly deteriorate until haemostasis is no longer possible.[10]

Initial management of major PPH

The management of a major PPH requires the rapid initiation of multiple overlapping actions. The exact sequence will be dictated by the needs of the individual mother and the resources available.

An outline of the initial management for a major postpartum haemorrhage is shown in Figure 6.1. This is discussed in more detail in the following section.

Major PPH is a serious obstetric emergency. Blood loss can become torrential and the mother's condition can quickly deteriorate. Remember that blood loss is often underestimated and may be concealed.

CALL FOR HELP

Activate the emergency buzzer to summon assistance and emergency bleep appropriate personnel:

- senior midwife
- experienced obstetrician
- additional support staff
- consultant obstetrician
- consultant anaesthetist
- porter ready to take urgent samples.

Alert the haematologist, blood bank technician and theatre staff to be on stand-by as the Code Red Major Obstetric Haemorrhage protocol may be activated.

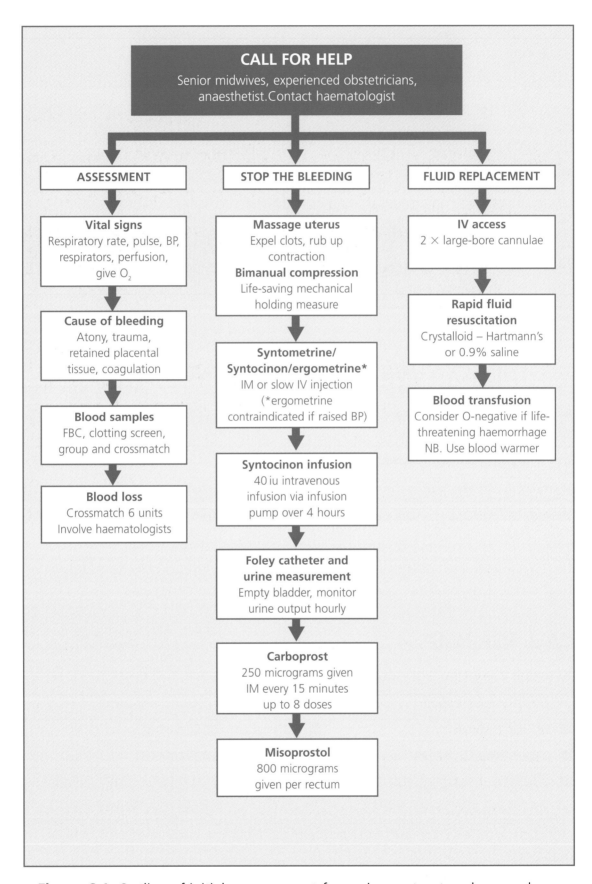

Figure 6.1. Outline of initial management for major postpartum haemorrhage

PPH emergency box

Many units have a PPH emergency box (Figure 6.2) containing emergency equipment, treatment algorithms and medication required for the immediate management of PPH.

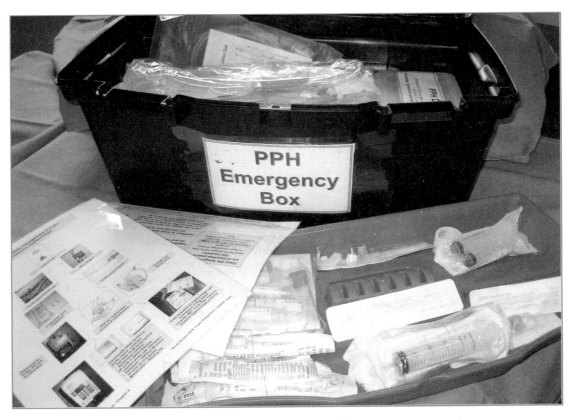

Figure 6.2. The postpartum haemorrhage emergency box

ASSESSMENT – rapid evaluation

Quickly assess the overall condition of the mother. This includes:

- respiratory rate and oxygen saturations, pulse, blood pressure
- peripheral perfusion
- abdominal palpation
- catheterise and monitor urine output
- estimation of blood loss: weigh swabs, incontinence pads, etc.
- urgent blood samples: FBC, U&Es, coagulation studies, crossmatch 6 units of blood and ask haematologist to send group specific blood until crossmatched blood available.
- Use O-negative blood (from labour ward fridge) if life-threatening haemorrhage.

Observe for signs of shock. A maternal tachycardia of greater than 100 beats/minute, a respiratory rate of over 30 breaths/minute and peripheral vasoconstriction indicates significant blood loss with initial physiological compensation (see Table 6.1). If the systolic blood pressure falls to less than 100 mmHg, the blood loss is likely to be at least 25% of the maternal blood volume.

- Check whether the uterus is well contracted.
- Check that the placenta has been expelled and is complete.
- Examine the cervix, vagina and perineum for tears.
- Observe for signs of clotting disorders, such as oozing from wound sites.
- Employ initial measures to treat shock. Give high-flow facial oxygen via a rebreather mask and autotransfuse by elevation of the mother's legs and/or head down tilt.
- Continuing monitoring: use high-dependency chart. Record observations at 15-minute intervals, hourly urine output, consider CVP, arterial lines, liaise with anaesthetist.

STOP THE BLEEDING

Remember that there may be more than one cause for the bleeding.

Massage the uterus

Remember that the most common cause of PPH is uterine atony. Check that the uterus is well contracted – it should feel 'like a cricket ball'. If the uterus is flaccid, 'rub up' a contraction. Expel any blood clots trapped in the uterus, as these inhibit effective uterine contractions. Use bimanual compression if bleeding continues.

Bimanual compression of uterus

If the bleeding continues, perform bimanual compression of the uterus as shown in Figure 6.3.

Insert a hand into the vagina, form a fist and place it in the anterior fornix. Apply pressure against the anterior wall of the uterus and, with the other hand, press deeply into the abdomen behind the uterus to apply pressure against the posterior wall of the uterus. Maintain compression until bleeding is controlled and the uterus contracts. This is particularly suitable for use in a domiciliary setting, or when the woman is on the postnatal ward as an effective mechanical holding measure until arrival on the labour ward.

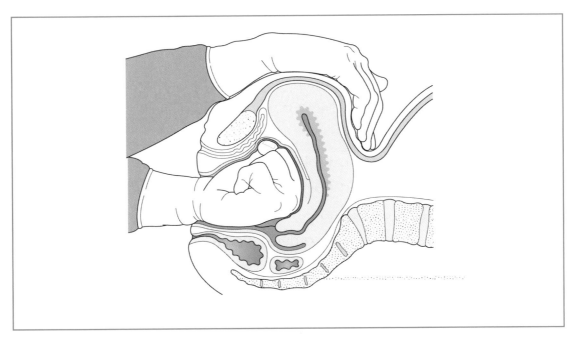

Figure 6.3. Bimanual compression of the uterus

First-line drug therapy

Treatment combinations may include administering intramuscular Syntometrine (oxytocin 5 iu and ergometrine 0.5 mg) if there is no immediate intravenous access and no maternal hypertension. The intramuscular route is an acceptable holding measure while awaiting help, although drug absorption will be less effective if there is peripheral shutdown. A second dose of Syntometrine intramuscularly may be considered if there is delay in obtaining intravenous access or if major haemorrhage occurs at a home delivery.

If intravenous access is already established give a bolus of 5 iu Syntocinon by slow intravenous injection, then a further 5 iu may be given if needed. Consider the use of antiemetics such as metoclopramide hydrochloride 10 mg, to counteract adverse effects such as nausea and vomiting.

Commence an intravenous infusion of oxytocin (Syntocinon 40 iu diluted in 500 ml physiological saline and infused via an infusion pump at 125 ml/hour over 4 hours).

Note that ergometrine is contraindicated in the presence of maternal hypertension. In addition, bolus doses of intravenous Syntocinon should be used with caution when there is extreme maternal hypotension, as it can cause a further fall in blood pressure.[2]

Catheterise the bladder

A full bladder can inhibit effective contraction of the uterus. Insert an indwelling Foley's catheter to empty the bladder. Note the amount drained and monitor further urinary output hourly as an indicator of renal function.

Repair the tear

Tears of the birth canal can be a source of significant blood loss and are the second most frequent cause of PPH. Apply pressure as an initial holding measure. Stabilise the mother and repair the tears or lacerations as soon as possible, ensuring adequate analgesia and good lighting. This woman would normally be transferred to theatre, as a full examination under anaesthesia is often required.

FLUID REPLACMENT – restore circulating blood volume

Establish two intravenous infusions. Use large-bore cannulae (grey or brown). Take blood samples for crossmatch (minimum of 6 units), full blood count and clotting screen. Crystalloid solutions (for example, Hartmann's solution or 0.9% saline) are the first-line choice for early fluid replacement. Fluids should be infused as rapidly as possible until the systolic blood pressure has been restored. Physiological (normal) 0.9% saline should be avoided in mothers with pre-eclampsia or liver disease, as sodium overload can occur so Hartmann's solution should be used.

Dextrans should not be used in obstetric practice as they interfere with blood tests, platelet function and have been associated with anaphylactic reactions and sudden fetal demise.[11]

An infusion of 1000 ml crystalloid will only increase plasma volume by about 200 ml, as around 80% of the infused solution will move outside the intravascular space. The amount of fluid administered must therefore be three to four times the estimated blood loss.

Peripheral oedema can occur when mothers receive large volumes of crystalloid but this should not be equated with the presence of pulmonary oedema. Crystalloids are easily excreted if excess fluid administration results in hypervolaemia; diuresis can be enhanced with furosemide.

Choice of intravenous fluids

A systematic review of randomised trials compared crystalloid and colloid solution for volume replacement in critically ill patients.[12] The use of colloids (for example, Haemaccel®, KoRa, or Gelofusine®, Braun) was associated with an increase in mortality of 4% compared with crystalloids; that is, four extra deaths for every 100 patients resuscitated. Colloids were not associated with improved survival and were more expensive than crystalloids so their continued use should be questioned.

If colloids are given, the volume should not exceed 1000–1500 ml in 24 hours, as larger amounts can have adverse effects on haemostatic function.[13,14] It is important that the development of a dilutional coagulopathy is avoided if possible, by the early use of fresh frozen plasma (FFP) and other blood products as required.[1]

Give blood and blood products

Both blood volume and oxygen carrying capacity need to be restored. Compatible blood should be transfused as soon as possible (using a blood warmer or rapid infuser). It is preferable to give blood of the same group as the mother. However, if compatible blood is not available after 3.5 litres of clear intravenous fluids have been given or if the bleeding is massive and unrelenting, then transfuse with uncrossmatched O-negative blood.

FFP, platelet concentrate and cryoprecipitate should be given after consideration of clotting study results or clinical impression. However, after infusing 6 units of 'plasma-free' red cells, it is highly probable that coagulation will be sufficiently disrupted such that clotting factors will need to be replaced. FFP and platelet concentrate, contain all coagulation components: Therefore, the haematologist should be contacted early for advice on treatment.

- If clotting time is prolonged or clinically indicated, infuse FFP.
- If platelet count is below 50×10^9 or clinically indicated, give platelet concentrates (remember that these must be kept at room temperature and agitated and once allocated cannot be used elsewhere).
- If coagulation tests are not corrected by FFP, give cryoprecipitate. This is used when a more concentrated source of fibrinogen is required.

> ## Immediate management key points
>
> - Early involvement of senior staff – obstetric, midwifery, anaesthetic, haematology.
> - Rapid assessment – observe for signs of shock.
> - Adequate venous access.
> - Stop the bleeding – oxytocics, mechanical measures.
> - Rapid fluid resuscitation with crystalloid until compatible blood is available.
> - Transfuse with compatible blood and blood products as soon as possible.
> - Use uncrossmatched O-negative blood if compatible blood is not available or the haemorrhage is torrential.

Continuing management of postpartum haemorrhage

Observe and evaluate the mother's condition and response to initial measures.

Intensive monitoring

Commence continuous monitoring of respirations, pulse rate, blood pressure and oxygenation. Chart observations, fluid balance and document initial management and treatment plan on a high-dependency chart.

Central venous pressure monitoring at an early stage, to guide fluid replacement, has been emphasised in Confidential Enquiries into Maternal Deaths. This may be particularly useful when major haemorrhage occurs in a woman with pre-eclampsia, where there is a fine balance between fluid replacement and fluid overload.

Unrelenting haemorrhage

Carboprost

Unrelenting haemorrhage is a significant threat to the life of the mother. If the uterus continues to relax despite initial measures, give carboprost

(Hemabate®, Pharmacia) 250 micrograms by deep intramuscular injection. This can be repeated at 15-minute intervals (to a maximum of eight doses). Intramyometrial injection is quicker acting and can be given through the abdominal wall. It can be injected directly into the myometrium at laparotomy. Adverse effects are uncommon but carboprost can induce vomiting, diarrhoea, headache, hypertension and bronchospasm. Use with caution in mothers with cardiac, pulmonary, renal or hepatic disorders.

Note: prostaglandins can be fatal if given intravenously.

Other drugs

The use of rectal misoprostol (800 micrograms given rectally) has been described. Misoprostol is a synthetic analogue of prostaglandin E1 and has the advantage of being thermostable and inexpensive. In a recent meta-analysis,[15] rectal misoprostol was found to be superior to a combination of intramuscular Syntometrine and oxytocic infusion in the subjective cessation of bleeding within 20 minutes. However, this was based on one small study of 64 women and the authors concluded that the evidence was insufficient to support replacing the oxytocin/ergometrine combination with misoprostol in the treatment of primary postpartum haemorrhage. Further research is needed to identify the optimum combination and dosage of uterotonic drugs.

Treat coagulopathies

When major haemorrhage occurs, one of the primary aims is to prevent the development of DIC by early involvement of the haematologist and prompt use of warmed blood and blood products. However, if DIC is suspected, laboratory tests are essential for diagnosis and the haematology department must be fully involved in the woman's management and treatment. Treatment consists of platelets, fresh frozen plasma and/or cryoprecipitate.[10] If bleeding cannot be surgically controlled, it may be necessary to begin treatment before the results of a coagulation screen are available.

Recombinant factor VIIa

Recombinant factor VIIa was originally developed for patients with haemophilia. It induces haemostasis by enhancing thrombin generation and providing the formation of a stable fibrin clot which is resistant to premature fibrinolysis. Subsequently, it was used for massive intraoperative haemorrhages.

The first obstetric report was in 2001 and there have been more than 65 case reports since, which were recently reviewed by Franchini et al. in 2007.[16] Patients responded to treatment with recombinant factor VIIa in 62/65 cases and 73% required only one dose. The recommended dose is 40–60 micrograms/kg. The reviewers advise a cautious interpretation of these results as there are no controls and there is a likely publication bias. There are also reports of a higher rate of thromboembolic events in the patients who received it. Therefore it should be used, only after consultation with the haematologist.

Uterine packing/tamponade

Uterine packing/tamponade involves packing the uterine cavity with mesh gauze, which is sometimes inserted inside a sterile plastic drape for easier removal. Special instruments can be used to introduce the packing but they are not mandatory. It is packing the uterus completely and uniformly that is important. There is no fixed interval for removal of the packing; it is usually removed after 24–36 hours. The evidence from many case reports over several decades suggests that this technique can be useful in the control of haemorrhage, with few reports of infection or adverse events.[17]

Uterine balloon tamponade has also been reported to be an effective measure. Johanson et al.[18] reported successful control of PPH using a Rusch hydrostatic balloon catheter. The technique comprises:

- catheterising the bladder (indwelling Foley)
- putting mother in Lloyd Davis position
- using a weighted speculum to access the vagina
- inserting Rusch balloon into the uterine cavity
- inflating the balloon with 400–500 ml of warm saline
- leaving the Rusch catheter in place for 24 hours
- continuing oxytocin infusion to maintain uterine contractions.

The use of this method has been described as the 'tamponade' test.[19] If the 'tamponade' test fails to stop the bleeding (following vaginal delivery), a laparotomy will probably be necessary.

Aortic compression

This is a mechanical holding measure, which can be used while further treatment is organised. The aorta is compressed against the spine. A closed fist is used to apply downward pressure over the abdominal aorta just above and slightly to the left of the umbilicus (Figure 6.4). The femoral pulse should be obliterated if the compression is adequate. This method can also be employed if the postpartum haemorrhage occurs during a caesarean section.

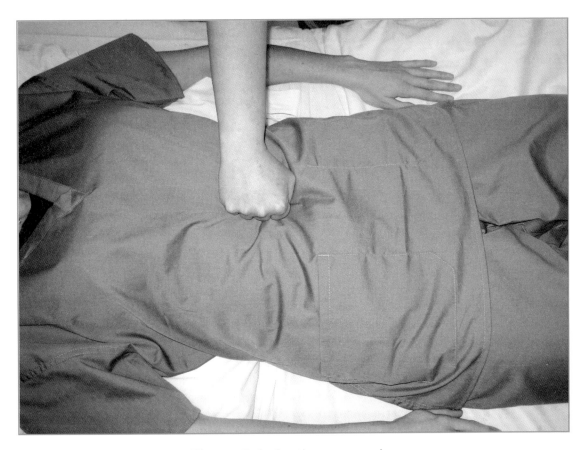

Figure 6.4. Aortic compression

Early recourse to surgical measures

If further bleeding occurs, transfer the mother to theatre for examination under anaesthesia and possible laparotomy.

Exploration of the uterus/laparotomy

Persistent uterine atony may be caused by retained placental tissue or blood clots and exploration of the uterus should be performed as soon as the mother has been resuscitated. Bimanual compression and aortic compression, as previously described, can be used as a holding measure at time of laparotomy.

The NICE intrapartum care guideline states that no particular surgical procedure can be recommended above another for the treatment of postpartum haemorrhage.[20]

B-Lynch suture and other compression measures

The B-Lynch 'brace suture' may be a useful alternative to hysterectomy. The technique was first described in 1997 and is simple and effective with successful outcomes in a number of case reports.[21] A simple diagram of the technique is shown in Figure 6.5. In the 2004 Confidential Enquiry into Maternal Deaths in the UK, no deaths were reported in those women who had a B-Lynch suture.[1] However, in the survey by UKOSS, 50/318 peripartum hysterectomies performed in the UK were preceded by an unsuccessful B-Lynch or other brace suture.[3,4]

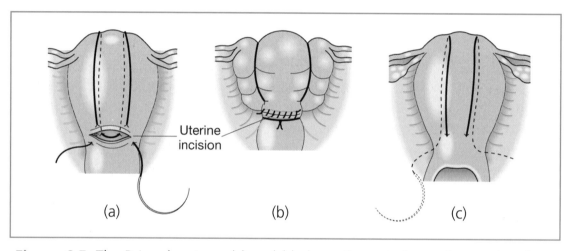

Figure 6.5. The B-Lynch suture: (a) and (c) show the anterior and posterior views of the uterus showing the application of the brace suture; (b) shows the anatomical appearance after complete application (original illustration by Mr Philip Wilson FMAA AIMI, based on the author's video record of the operation; reproduced with permission from *Br J Obstet Gynaecol* 1997;104:374)

The original description of the technique requires the uterine cavity to be opened and explored and a bimanual compression test employed prior to insertion of the suture. If bimanual compression is ineffective in reducing the bleeding, then the B-Lynch suture is unlikely to be successful.

More recently, there have been many modifications of the B-Lynch suture described in literature. They all follow the same principle of compressing the uterus to stop the bleeding. Some techniques do not require opening of the uterine cavity, while others describe parallel or vertical sutures that compress the anterior uterine wall against the posterior wall.[22–24] Most of the published series have favourable outcomes with many subsequent pregnancies reported in the same woman.

Uterine vessel ligation

Uterine vessel ligation was first described by Waters in 1952.[25] Case series have reported high success rates in the control of haemorrhage and low rates of complications.[26]

The uterine artery and vein are ligated, at the level of the uppermost part of the lower uterine segment. An atraumatic needle is passed 2–3 cm medially to the vessels, to include 2–3 cm of myometrium. The needle is brought through the broad ligament lateral to the vessels. Ligation of the ovarian (infudibulopelvic) vessels may be performed if the bleeding continues.

Internal iliac artery ligation

The technique involves identifying the bifurcation of the common iliac artery, where the ureter crosses it. A longitudinal 4–5 cm incision is made in the pelvic peritoneum at the level of the bifurcation of the common iliac artery, inferior and lateral to the ureter. The ureter is then retracted medially and the artery is ligated 2.5 cm distal to the bifurcation of internal and external iliac artery. Appropriate non-absorbable suture material is fed around the artery and two free ligatures tied 1.5–2.0 cm apart. The operation results in a reduction in the pulse pressure distal to the ligation.[27] Trauma to the iliac veins should be avoided. The vessel is not divided and the external iliac artery and femoral pulse should be identified after ligation. The assistance of a vascular surgeon should be considered for those inexperienced in the technique. Joshi *et al.* reported a series of 110 internal iliac ligations for postpartum haemorrhage.[28] In their series, internal iliac artery ligation was more effective for cases of uterine atony and placenta praevia (hysterectomy rates 36% and 14%, respectively), rather than cases of uterine rupture where the hysterectomy rate was 79%.

Hysterectomy

Hysterectomy may be necessary if bleeding persists but the decision should be made and the procedure carried out by a consultant. This course of action should not be delayed by attempts with unfamiliar techniques.

Placenta praevia, particularly in mothers with a previous uterine scar, may be associated with uncontrollable uterine haemorrhage at delivery and caesarean hysterectomy may be necessary. A highly experienced operator is essential and a consultant must be readily available.

When a placenta accreta is found, attempts at removal should be abandoned and, if severe bleeding persists, peripartum hysterectomy should be considered. If there is no bleeding, there is the option of conservative management. The placenta is left in place and postoperative ultrasound and serial blood test monitoring are employed until placental reabsorption is shown.[29]

Unrelenting haemorrhage is probably one of the most testing situations for all professionals involved. While the decision to perform a hysterectomy is never taken lightly it is important not to delay this course of action until the mother is nearly moribund.

Massive obstetric haemorrhage protocol

All maternity units should have a Code Red Obstetric Haemorrhage protocol for cases of massive haemorrhage. The multiprofessional team should update and rehearse this protocol regularly in conjunction with haematology and blood bank.[1,8]

Continuing management key points
■ Intensive monitoring.
■ Carboprost by deep intramuscular or intramyometrial injection.
■ Watch out for consumptive coagulopathy.
■ Use manual holding measures while arranging further treatment.
■ Early recourse to surgical intervention.
■ Aftercare in high-dependency or intensive care unit.

References

1. Lewis G, editor. *Saving Mothers' Lives: reviewing maternal deaths to make motherhood safer 2003–2005. The Seventh Report of the Confidential Enquiries into Maternal Deaths in the United Kingdom*. London: CEMACH; 2007.

2. Lewis G, editor. *Why Mothers Die 2000–2002: Sixth Report on Confidential Enquiries into Maternal Deaths in the United Kingdom*. London: RCOG Press; 2004.

3. Stones RW, Paterson CM, Saunders NStG. Risk factors for major obstetric haemorrhage. *Eur J Obstet Gynecol Reprod Biol* 1993;48:15–18.

4. Bonnar J. Massive obstetric haemorrhage. *Balliere's Best Pract Res Clin Obstet Gynaecol* 2000;14:1–18.

5. Drife J. Management of primary postpartum haemorrhage. *Br J Obstet Gynaecol* 1997;104:275–7.

6. McDonald S, Prendiville WJ, Elbourne D. Prophylactic syntometrine versus oxytocin for delivery of the placenta. *Cochrane Database Syst Rev* 2001;(4).

7. Prendiville WJ, Elbourne D, McDonald S. Active versus expectant management in the third stage of labour. *Cochrane Database Syst Rev* 2001;(4).

8. UK Obstetric Surveillance System [www.npeu.ox.ac.uk/UKOSS].

9. Knight M. Peripartum hysterectomy in the UK: study of a 'near-miss' event using the UK Obstetric Surveillance System (UKOSS). Abstract presented at the British International Congress of Obstetrics and Gynaecology, July 2007 [www.npeu.ox.ac.uk/UKOSS/ukoss_downloads/BCOG_PH_abstract_160107.pdf].

10. Stainsby D, MacLennan S, Hamilton P. Management of massive blood loss a template guide. *Br J Anaesth* 2000;85:487–91.

11. Berg EM, Fasting S, Sellevold OF. Serious complications with dextran-70 despite hapten prophylaxis. Is it best avoided prior to delivery? *Anaesthesia* 1991;91:1033–5.

12. Schierhout G, Roberts I. Fluid resuscitation with colloid or crystalloid solutions in critically ill patients: a systematic review of randomised trials. *Br Med J* 1998;316:961–4.

13. Hewitt PE, Machin SJ. Massive blood transfusion In: *ABC of Transfusion*. London. BMJ Publishing Group; 1998. p. 49–52.

14. Hippala S. Replacement of massive blood loss. *Vox Sanguinis* 1998;74:399–407.

15 Mousa HA, Alfirevic Z. Treatment of primary postpartum haemorrhage. *Cochrane Database Syst Rev* 2007;(1).

16. Franchini M, Lippi G, Franchi M. The use of rFVIIa in obstetric and gynaecological haemorrhage. *BJOG* 2007;114:8–15.

17. Maier RC. Control of postpartum haemorrhage with uterine packing. *Am J Obstet Gynecol* 1993;169:317–23.

18. Johanson R, Kumar M, Obhrai M, Young P. Management of massive postpartum haemorrhage: use of hydrostatic balloon catheter to avoid laparotomy. *BJOG* 2001;108:420–2.

19. Condous GS, Arulkumaran S, Symonds I, Chapman R, Sinha A, Razvi K. The 'tamponade test' in the management of massive postpartum haemorrhage. *Obstet Gynecol* 2003;101:767–72.

20. National Collaborating Centre for Women's and Children's Health. *Intrapartum Care: care of healthy women and their babies during childbirth. Clinical guideline*. London: RCOG Press; 2007.

21. B-Lynch C, Coker A, Adegboyega HL, Abu J, Cowen MJ. The B-Lynch surgical technique for the control of massive postpartum haemorrhage: an alternative to hysterectomy? Five cases reported. *Br J Obstet Gynaecol* 1997;104:372–5.

22. Hayman RG, Arulkumaran S, Steer PJ. Uterine compression sutures: surgical management of postpartum hemorrhage. *Obstet Gynecol* 2002;99:502–6.

23. Hwu YM, Chen CP, Chen HS, Su TH. Parallel vertical compression sutures; a technique to control bleeding from placenta praevia or accreta during caesarean section. *BJOG* 2005;112:1420–3.

24. Ouahba J, Piketty M, Huel C, Azarian M, Feraud O, Luton D, *et al*. Uterine compression sutures for postpartum bleeding with uterine atony. *BJOG* 2007;114:619–22.

25. Waters E. Surgical management of postpartum haemorrhage with particular reference to ligation of uterine arteries. *Am J Obstet Gynecol* 1952;64:1143–8.

26. O'Learly JA. Uterine artery ligation for control of caesarean haemorrhage. *J Reprod Med* 1995;40:189–93.

27. Cunningham E, Leveno KJ, Bloom SL, Hauth JC, Gilstrap LC, Wenstrom KD. *Williams Obstetrics.* 21st ed. London: McGraw-Hill; 2001.

28. Joshi V, Otiv S, Majumder R, Nikam Y, Shrivastava M. Internal iliac artery ligation for arresting postpartum haemorrhage. *BJOG* 2007;114: 356-61.

29. Kayem G, Davy C, Goffinet F, Thomas C, Clement D, Cabrol D. Conservative versus extirpative management in cases of placenta accreta. *Obstet Gynecol* 2004;104:531–6.

Module 7
Shoulder dystocia

Key learning points

- Antenatal and intrapartum risk factors.
- Understand manoeuvres required to effect delivery during shoulder dystocia.
- Clear and accurate documentation.
- Awareness of potential complications of shoulder dystocia.

Common difficulties observed in training drills

- Not calling the neonatologist.
- Not clearly stating the problem.
- Inability to gain appropriate internal vaginal access.
- Confusion over internal rotational manoeuvres.
- Resorting to traction to effect delivery.
- Use of fundal pressure instead of suprapubic pressure.

Introduction

Definition

Shoulder dystocia is when additional manoeuvres (such as McRoberts' position and suprapubic pressure) are required to complete the delivery of the fetus, after routine downward traction has failed to deliver the shoulders during a normal vaginal delivery.[1]

Incidence

Shoulder dystocia complicates approximately 1% of all vaginal deliveries.[2]

Pathophysiology

When shoulder dystocia occurs, the fetal body is prevented from delivering after the head because the anterior fetal shoulder impacts on the maternal symphysis pubis. Less commonly, the posterior fetal shoulder impacts on the maternal sacral promontory.

Risk factors for shoulder dystocia

A number of antenatal and intrapartum characteristics have been reported to be associated with shoulder dystocia (Box 7.1) but even a combination of risk factors is poorly predictive.[2]

Box 7.1. Risk factors for shoulder dystocia	
Prelabour	**Intrapartum**
Previous shoulder dystocia	Prolonged first stage
Macrosomia	Prolonged second stage
Maternal diabetes mellitus	Labour augmentation
Maternal obesity	Instrumental delivery

Previous shoulder dystocia is a risk factor for recurrent shoulder dystocia. The recurrence rate of shoulder dystocia is reported to be at least 10%.[3] However, this may be an underestimate, as women who have had shoulder dystocia in a previous delivery may have opted for caesarean section in their subsequent pregnancies.

Macrosomia

Large fetal size increases the risk of shoulder dystocia: the greater the fetal birth weight, the higher the risk of shoulder dystocia. A review of 14 721 births reported rates of shoulder dystocia in non-diabetic mothers of: 1% in infants weighing less than 4000 g, 10% in infant weighing 4000–4499 g and 23% in infants weighing more than 4500 g.[4] However, macrosomia remains a weak predictor of shoulder dystocia. The large majority of infants with a birth weight of greater than 4500 g do not develop shoulder dystocia and up to 50% of cases of shoulder dystocia occur in infants with a birth weight less than 4000 g.[5,6] Furthermore, antenatal detection of macrosomia is poor: third-trimester ultrasound scans have at least a 10% margin for error of actual birth weight and detect only 60% of infants weighing over 4500 g.[7]

Maternal diabetes mellitus

Maternal diabetes increases the risk of shoulder dystocia.[8] For the same birth weight, infants of mothers with diabetes have a three to four times greater risk of shoulder dystocia compared with infants of mothers without diabetes. This is probably due to the different body shape of babies of diabetic mothers.[4]

Instrumental delivery

There is a higher rate of shoulder dystocia following instrumental delivery than with normal vaginal delivery.[9]

Obesity

Women with a raised body mass index (BMI) are at higher risk of shoulder dystocia than women with a normal BMI.[10] However, women who are obese tend to have larger babies and the association between maternal obesity and shoulder dystocia is therefore likely to be due to fetal macrosomia, rather than the maternal obesity itself.[11]

> ### Key points
>
> - The majority of cases of shoulder dystocia occur in women with no risk factors.
> - Shoulder dystocia is therefore an unpredictable and largely unpreventable event.
> - Clinicians should be aware of existing risk factors but must always be alert to the possibility of shoulder dystocia with any delivery.

Prevention

Shoulder dystocia can only be prevented by caesarean section. However, even in the presence of suspected fetal macrosomia, elective caesarean section is not recommended as a method of reducing potential morbidity from possible shoulder dystocia. It has been estimated that an additional 2345 caesarean deliveries would be required to prevent one permanent injury from shoulder dystocia.[7]

The only clinical circumstance when elective caesarean section is recommended is for women with diabetes and suspected fetal macrosomia or where the estimated fetal weight is greater than 5 kg in a woman without diabetes.[12] This is because of the higher incidence of shoulder dystocia and brachial plexus injury in this subgroup.

Management

There are numerous manoeuvres that can be used to resolve shoulder dystocia. The RCOG evidenced-based algorithm for the management of shoulder dystocia is shown in Figure 7.1. This is described in detail in the next section.

There is no evidence that one intervention is superior to another; therefore, the algorithm begins with simple measures that are often effective and leads progressively to manoeuvres that are more invasive. Variations in the sequence of actions may be appropriate.

Recognition of shoulder dystocia

- There may be difficulty with delivery of the face and chin.
- When the head is delivered, it remains tightly applied to the vulva.

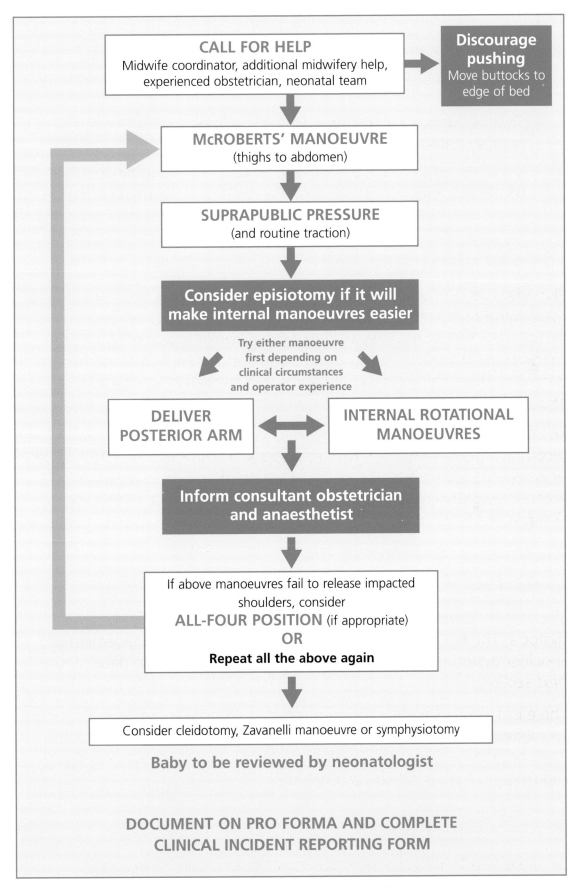

Figure 7.1. Algorithm for the management of shoulder dystocia

- The chin retracts and depresses the perineum – the 'turtle-neck' sign.
- The anterior shoulder fails to deliver with routine traction.

Call for help

- Use the emergency buzzer (not the call bell).
- Call for:
  - ☐ senior midwife
  - ☐ additional midwifery staff
  - ☐ most experienced obstetrician available
  - ☐ neonatologist.
- Remember to call for the neonatologist – this is often forgotten during attempted delivery.
- Consider calling the obstetric consultant and an anaesthetist.

Clearly state the problem. Announce 'Shoulder dystocia' as help arrives.

Note the time the head was delivered (start the clock on the resuscitaire or mark CTG, if monitoring).

Ask the mother to stop pushing. Pushing should be discouraged, as it may increase the risk of neurological and orthopaedic complications and will not resolve the dystocia.

McRoberts' manoeuvre

Lie the mother flat and remove any pillows from under her back. Bring her to the end of the bed or remove the end of the bed to make vaginal access easier. With one assistant on either side, hyperflex the mother's legs against her abdomen so that her knees are up towards her ears (Figure 7.2). If the mother is in the lithotomy position, her legs will need to be removed from the supports to achieve McRoberts' positioning. Routine traction (the same degree of traction applied during a normal delivery) should then be applied to the baby's head to assess whether the shoulders have been released.

If the anterior shoulder is not released with McRoberts' position, move on to the next manoeuvre. Do not continue to apply traction to the baby's head.

Remember: shoulder dystocia is a 'bony problem' where the baby's shoulder is obstructed by the mother's pelvis. If the entrapment is not released by McRoberts' position, another manoeuvre (not traction) is required to free the shoulder and achieve delivery.

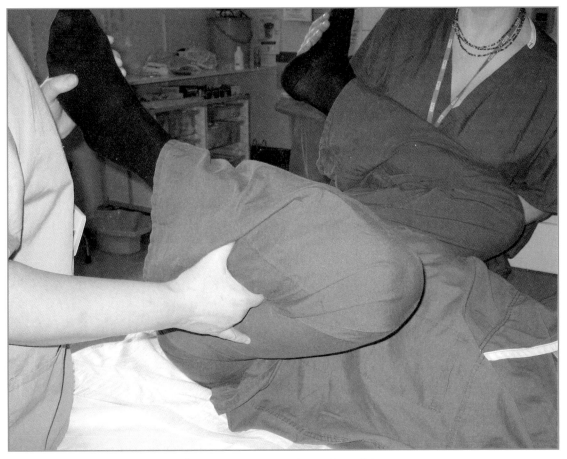

Figure 7.2. McRoberts' position

McRoberts' position increases the relative anteroposterior diameter of the pelvic inlet by rotating the maternal pelvis cephaloid and straightening the sacrum relative to the lumbar spine. McRoberts' position is the single most effective intervention in shoulder dystocia management with reported success rates between 40% and 90%.[13]

McRoberts' position is not recommended as a prophylactic manoeuvre in anticipation of shoulder dystocia.

Suprapubic pressure

The aim of suprapubic pressure is to reduce the diameter of the fetal shoulders (the bisacromial diameter) and rotate the anterior shoulder into the wider oblique angle of the pelvis. The shoulder is then free to slip underneath the symphysis pubis.[14]

An assistant should perform suprapubic pressure from the side of the fetal back. Pressure is applied in a downward and lateral direction, just above the maternal symphysis pubis, to push the posterior aspect of the anterior

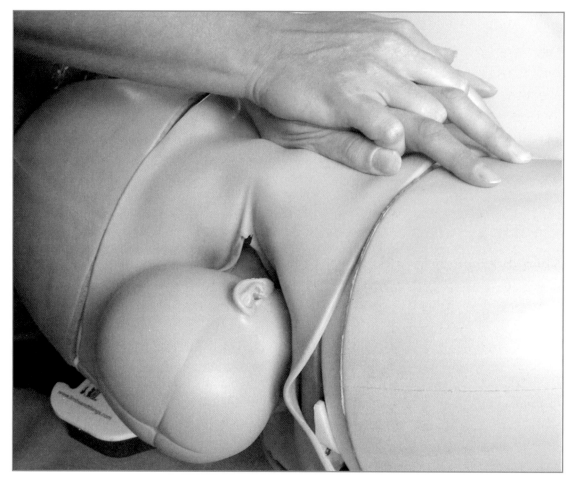

Figure 7.3. Applying suprapubic pressure

shoulder towards the fetal chest (Figure 7.3). There is no evidence that rocking is better than continuous pressure when performing suprapubic pressure, nor that it should be performed for 30 seconds for it to be effective. Only routine traction should be applied to the fetal head when assessing whether the manoeuvre has been successful. Again, if the anterior shoulder is not released with suprapubic pressure and routine traction move on to the next manoeuvre.

Evaluate the need for an episiotomy

An episiotomy will not relieve the bony obstruction of shoulder dystocia but may be required to allow the accoucheur more space to facilitate internal vaginal manoeuvres.[15] However, there may be enough room to gain internal access without performing an episiotomy. Often the perineum has already torn or an episiotomy may have already been performed before delivery of the head.

Internal manoeuvres

There are two categories of internal vaginal manoeuvres that can be performed if McRoberts' position and suprapubic pressure have not been effective – internal rotational manoeuvres and delivery of the posterior arm. There is no evidence demonstrating that either is superior or that one should attempted before the other but all internal manoeuvres start with the same action – inserting the whole hand posteriorly into the sacral hollow.

Gaining internal vaginal access

When shoulder dystocia occurs, the problem is usually at the inlet of the pelvis, with the anterior shoulder trapped above the symphysis pubis. The temptation, therefore, is to try to gain vaginal access anteriorly to perform manoeuvres. However, there is very little room underneath the pubic arch and therefore attempting any manoeuvre can be extremely difficult (Figure 7.4).

The most spacious part of the pelvis is in the sacral hollow; therefore vaginal access can be gained more easily posteriorly, into the sacral hollow. If the accoucheur scrunches up their hand (as if putting on a tight bracelet or reaching for the last Pringle® crisp in the bottom of the container), internal rotation or delivery of the posterior arm can then be attempted using their whole hand (Figure 7.5).

> Remember to ask for suprapubic pressure to be stopped while you gain internal vaginal access.

Delivery of the posterior arm

Delivering the posterior arm will reduce the diameter of the fetal shoulders by the width of the arm. This will usually provide enough room to resolve the shoulder dystocia.

Often, babies lie with their arms flexed across their chest and so, as your hand enters the vagina posteriorly, you will feel the fetal hand and forearm of the posterior arm (Figure 7.6). In this case, take hold of fetal wrist (with your fingers and thumb) and gently pull the posterior arm out in a straight line (Figure 7.7). Once the posterior arm is delivered (Figure 7.8), apply gentle traction to the fetal head. If the shoulder dystocia has resolved, the baby should then be easily delivered. However if, despite delivering the posterior arm, the shoulder dystocia has not resolved, support the head and

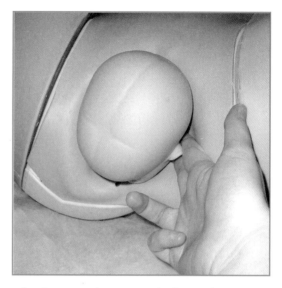

a. Attempting to gain anterior access

b. Attempting to gain lateral access

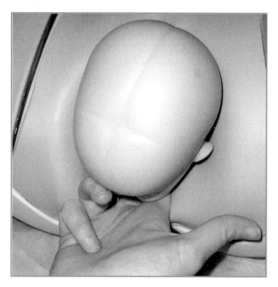

c. Entering the vagina with two fingers as if performing a routine vaginal examination

d. Leaving the thumb out of the vagina

Figure 7.4. Incorrect attempts at gaining vaginal access

posterior arm and gently rotate the baby through 180 degrees. The posterior shoulder will then become the new anterior shoulder and should be below the symphysis pubis, thus resolving the dystocia.

If the baby is lying with its posterior arm straight against its body, rather than a flexed posterior arm, this is much more difficult to deliver. In this situation, it may be easier to perform internal rotational manoeuvres

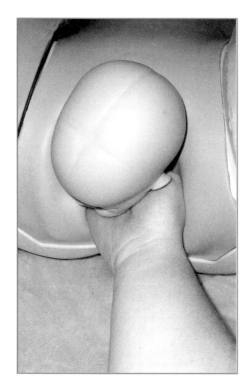

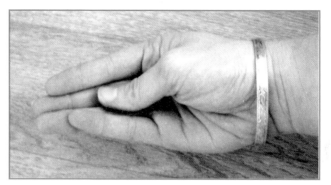

Figure 7.5. Correct vaginal access

instead, as the straight arm will need to be flexed so that the wrist can be grasped. This can be done by the accoucheur following the straight posterior arm down to the elbow, placing their thumb in the antecubital fossa and then applying pressure with their fingers to the back of the forearm just below the elbow. This should flex the posterior arm. The wrist can then be grasped and the arm delivered as previously described. If you can not reach the wrist, it is best not to pull on the upper arm as this is likely to result in a humeral fracture.

Internal rotational manoeuvres

The aims of internal rotation are:

- to move the fetal shoulders (the bisacromial diameter) out of the narrowest diameter of the mother's pelvis (the anterior–posterior) and into a wider pelvic diameter (the oblique or transverse)
- to reduce the fetal bisacromial diameter
- to use the maternal pelvic anatomy: as the fetal shoulders are rotated within the mother's pelvis the fetal shoulder descends through the pelvis due to the bony architecture of the pelvis.

Figure 7.6.
Location of
the posterior
arm

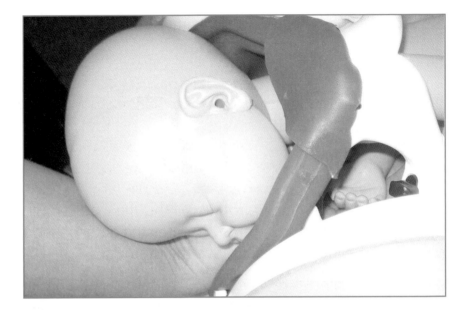

Figure 7.7.
Grasp the
wrist of the
posterior arm

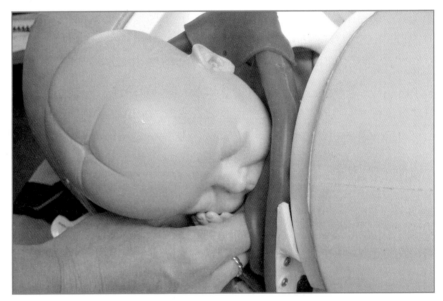

Figure 7.8.
Gentle
traction on
the posterior
arm in a
straight line

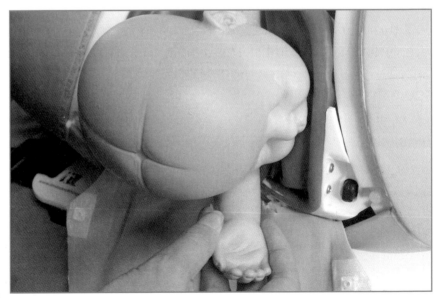

Internal rotational manoeuvres were originally described by Woods and Rubin. Rotation can be most easily achieved by pressing on the anterior (front) or posterior (back) aspect of the posterior (lowermost) shoulder (Figure 7.9). Pressure on the posterior aspect of the posterior shoulder has the added benefit of reducing the shoulder diameter by adducting the shoulders (scrunching the shoulders inwards). Rotation should move the shoulders into the wider oblique diameter, resolving the shoulder dystocia, so that delivery is possible with routine traction. If delivery does not occur continue the pressure and, by swapping hands, rotate the shoulders a complete turn (180-degree rotation). This manoeuvre (as with rotation after delivery of the posterior arm) substitutes the anterior shoulder for the posterior shoulder and will resolve the dystocia.

If pressure in one direction has no effect, try to rotate the shoulders in the opposite direction by pressing on the other side of the fetal posterior shoulder (that is, change from pressing on the front of the baby's shoulder to the back of the baby's shoulder or vice versa). If you are struggling, try changing the hand you are using.

If pressure on the posterior shoulder is unsuccessful, apply pressure on the anterior fetal shoulder. This is more difficult, as it is hard to reach the anterior shoulder. From the sacral hollow, follow the fetal back up to the anterior shoulder. Apply pressure on the posterior aspect of the anterior shoulder to adduct and rotate the shoulders into the oblique diameter.

While attempting to rotate the fetal shoulders from the inside of the pelvis, you can instruct a colleague to perform suprapubic pressure to assist your rotation. Ensure that you are pushing with and not against each other.

All-fours position

Roll the mother on to her hands and knees so that the maternal weight lies evenly on the four limbs. This simple change of position may dislodge the anterior shoulder. The all-fours position may also facilitate access to the posterior shoulder to enable internal manoeuvres to be performed. It may be difficult for some mothers to assume this position, particularly with an epidural block.

All-fours positioning was popularised by the midwife Ina May Gaskin. The evidence base is from voluntary notification of 82 selected cases of shoulder dystocia managed with the 'all-fours' position. The reported success rate was 83% without the need for additional manoeuvres and with few injuries to mother and babies.[16]

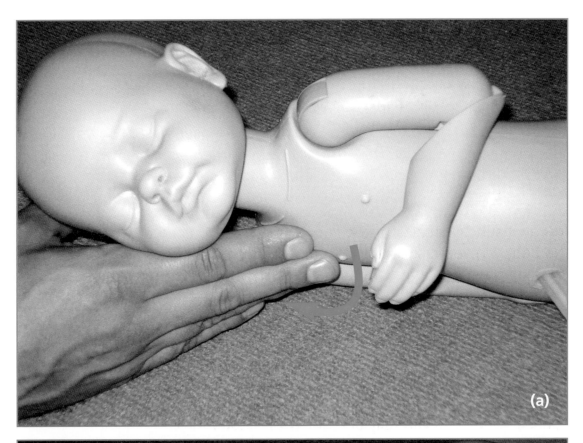

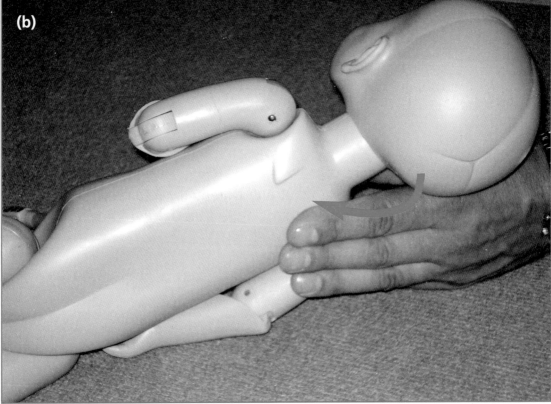

Figure 7.9. Internal rotational manoeuvres: (a) pressure on the anterior aspect of the posterior shoulder to achieve rotation; (b) pressure on posterior aspect of posterior shoulder to achieve rotation

Additional manoeuvres

In the UK, manoeuvres such as cephalic replacement (Zavanelli manoeuvre), symphysiotomy and cleidotomy (deliberate fracture of the clavicle) are uncommon. They are mainly considered as last-resort measures.

What to avoid

Traction

It is an instinctive reaction to pull on the fetal head in an attempt to deliver the baby. However, strong downward traction on the fetal head is associated with neonatal trauma, including permanent brachial plexus injury.[6] Traction will not resolve the dystocia and traction that is more forceful than that used during a normal delivery should not be used. There is also some evidence that traction applied quickly with a 'jerk', rather than applied slowly, may be more damaging to the nerves of the brachial plexus (imagine trying to snap a piece of cotton – it is much easier to break it with a quick pull than a slow one). Therefore, routine traction should always be applied slowly and carefully and not with sudden force.

Fundal pressure

Fundal pressure is associated with a high rate of brachial plexus injury and rupture of the uterus. It should therefore not be applied during shoulder dystocia.[17]

Documentation

Accurate documentation of a difficult and potentially traumatic delivery is essential. It may be helpful to use a pro forma to aid accurate record keeping. An example is provided in Figure 7.10.

It is important record:

- the time of delivery of the head
- the manoeuvres performed, the timing and sequence
- the traction applied
- the time of delivery of the body
- the staff in attendance and the time they arrived
- the condition of the baby

- umbilical cord blood acid-base measurements (cord pH)
- the anterior fetal shoulder at the time of the dystocia.

SHOULDER DYSTOCIA DOCUMENTATION

Date ....

Time ....

Person completing form ....

Signature ....

Mother's name _____

Date of birth _____

Hospital number _____

Consultant _____

Called for help at:		Emergency call via switchboard at:		
Staff present at delivery of head:		Additional staff attending		
Name	Grade	Name	Grade	Time arrived

Procedures used to assist delivery	By whom	Time	Order	Details	Reason if not performed
McRoberts' position					
Suprapubic pressure				From maternal **left / right**	
Episiotomy				Enough access / tear present / already performed	
Delivery of posterior arm					
Internal rotational manoeuvre					
Description of rotation					
Description of traction	Routine	Other:		Reason if not routine:	
Other manoeuvres used					

Time of delivery of head		Time of delivery of baby		Head-to-body delivery interval	
Fetal position during dystocia		Head facing maternal **left**		Head facing maternal **right**	
Birth weight	kg	Apgar score 1 minute:		5 minutes:	10 minutes:
Cord gases		Art pH :	Art BE:	Venous pH :	Venous BE :
Explanation to parents		Yes	No	Incident form completed	Yes	No

Figure 7.10. An example of a shoulder dystocia documentation pro forma

Parents

Shoulder dystocia is a frightening and potentially traumatic experience for the mother and her attending family. It is important to tell the parents what is happening and give the mother clear instructions during the emergency. Both the birth and the reason for the use of manoeuvres should be discussed after delivery.

Any baby with a suspected injury following shoulder dystocia should be immediately reviewed by a neonatologist. The Erb's Palsy Group is an excellent source of information and supports families and healthcare practitioners caring for children with brachial plexus injuries (www.erbspalsygroup.co.uk).

A woman who has had a previous shoulder dystocia should be referred to a consultant-led antenatal clinic in subsequent pregnancies to discuss antenatal care and mode of delivery.

Consequences of shoulder dystocia

Shoulder dystocia has a high perinatal morbidity and mortality.[13] Maternal morbidity is also increased (Box 7.2).

Box 7.2. Perinatal morbidity and mortality	
Perinatal	**Maternal**
Stillbirth	Postpartum haemorrhage
Hypoxia	Third- and fourth-degree tears
Brachial plexus injury	Uterine rupture
Fractures (humeral and clavicular)	Psychological distress

Acidosis

Shoulder dystocia is an acute life-threatening event. A review of 56 perinatal deaths attributed to shoulder dystocia found the median head-to-body delivery interval was 5 minutes.[18] A healthy fetus will compensate during shoulder dystocia but only for a finite amount of time. Babies may be born with a severe metabolic acidosis or may develop hypoxic ischaemic encephalopathy (HIE), with or without long-term neurological damage. The necessary resuscitation equipment should therefore be prepared and neonatal staff should be called as soon as shoulder dystocia occurs in case neonatal resuscitation is required.

Brachial plexus injury

Brachial plexus injury is one of the most important complications of shoulder dystocia and it affects approximately one in every 2300 deliveries in the UK.[19] The primary mechanism for brachial plexus injury is thought to be excessive traction on the fetal head during shoulder dystocia, although other mechanisms of injury have been proposed. Brachial plexus injury may be a complication of normal labour and has even been reported after caesarean section.[20] Injuries can be divided into upper (Erb's palsy), lower (Klumpke's palsy) or total brachial plexus injury:

- **Erb's palsy** is the most common injury. The upper arm is flaccid and the lower arm is extended and rotated towards the body with the hand held in a classic 'waiter's tip' posture. Up to 90% of Erb's palsies recover by 12 months.

- **Klumpke's palsy** is less common. The hand is limp, with no movement of the fingers. The recovery rate is lower and around 40% of injuries resolve by 12 months.

- **Total brachial plexus injury** occurs in approximately 20% of brachial plexus injuries.[21] There is a total sensory and motor deficit of the entire arm, making it completely paralysed with no sensation. Horner syndrome, caused by sympathetic nerve injury resulting in contraction of the pupil and ptosis of the eyelid on the affected side, may also be present. Full functional recovery is rare without surgical intervention. The prognosis is worse if Horner syndrome is present.[21]

Humeral and clavicular fractures

Humeral and clavicular fractures can also occur following shoulder dystocia. These fractures usually heal quickly and have a good prognosis.

Shoulder dystocia is an unpredictable obstetric emergency	
Problem	Clearly state the problem
Paediatrician	Immediately call the paediatrician/neonatologist
Pressure	Suprapubic (NOT FUNDAL) pressure
Posterior	Vaginal access gained posteriorly
Pringle®	Get the whole hand in
Pull	Don't keep pulling if a manoeuvre has not worked
Pro forma	Documentation should be clear and concise
Parents	Communication is essential

References

1. Resnick R. Management of shoulder dystocia girdle. *Clin Obstet Gynecol* 1980;23:559–64.

2. Ouzounian JG, Gherman RB. Shoulder dystocia: are historic risk factors reliable predictors? *Am J Obstet Gynecol* 2005;192:1933–5.

3. Ginsberg NA, Moisidis C. How to predict recurrent shoulder dystocia. *Am J Obstet Gynecol* 2001;184:1427–30.

4. Acker DB, Sachs BP, Friedman EA. Risk factors for shoulder dystocia. *Obstet Gynecol* 1985;66:762–8.

5. Naef RW 3rd, Martin JN Jr. Emergent management of shoulder dystocia. *Obstet Gynecol Clin North Am* 1995;22:247–59.

6. Baskett TF, Allen AC. Perinatal implications of shoulder dystocia. *Obstet Gynecol* 1995;86:14–17.

7. Rouse DJ, Owen J Prophylactic cesarean delivery for fetal macrosomia diagnosed by means of ultrasonography: a Faustian bargain? *Am J Obstet Gynecol* 1999;181:332–8.

8. Nesbitt TS, Gilbert WM, Herrchen B. Shoulder dystocia and associated risk factors with macrosomic infants born in California. *Am J Obstet Gynecol* 1998;179:476–80.

9. Benedetti TJ, Gabbe SG. Shoulder dystocia. A complication of fetal macrosomia and prolonged second stage of labor with midpelvic delivery. *Obstet Gynecol* 1978;52:526–9.

10. Sandmire HF, O'Halloin TJ. Shoulder dystocia: its incidence and associated risk factors. *Int J Gynaecol Obstet* 1988;26:65–73.

11. Usha Kiran TS, Hemmadi S, Bethel J, Evans J. Outcome of pregnancy in a woman with an increased body mass index. *BJOG* 2005;112:768–72.

12. Draycott TJ, Montague I, Fox R. *Shoulder Dystocia*. London, RCOG Press; 2005.

13. Gherman RB, Ouzounian JG, Goodwin TM. Obstetric maneuvers for shoulder dystocia and associated fetal morbidity. *Am J Obstet Gynecol* 1998;178:1126–30.

14. Lurie S, Ben-Arie A, Haqay Z. The ABC of shoulder dystocia management. *Asia Oceania J Obstet Gynaecol* 1994;20:195–7.

15. Hinshaw K. Shoulder dystocia. In: Grady K, Howell C, Cox C, editors. *Managing Obstetric Emergencies and Trauma: The MOET Course Manual*. 2nd ed. London, RCOG Press; 2007. p. 221–31.

16. Bruner JP, Drummond SB, Meenan AL, Gaskin IM. All-fours maneuver for reducing shoulder dystocia during labor. *J Reprod Med* 1998;43:439–43.

17. Gross TL, Sokol RJ, Williams T, Thompson K. Shoulder dystocia: a fetal-physician risk. *Am J Obstet Gynecol* 1987;156:1408–18.

18. Hope P, Breslin S, Lamont L, Lucas A, Martin D, Moore I, *et al*. Fatal shoulder dystocia: a review of 56 cases reported to the Confidential Enquiry into Stillbirths and Deaths in Infancy. *Br J Obstet Gynaecol* 1998;105:1256–61.

19. Evans-Jones G, Kay SP, Weindling AM, Cranny G, Ward A, Bradshaw A, *et al*. Congenital brachial palsy: incidence, causes, and outcome in the United Kingdom and Republic of Ireland. *Arch Dis Child Fetal Neonatal Ed* 2003;88:F185–9.

20. Allen RH, Bankoski BR, Butzin CA, Nagey DA. Comparing clinician-applied loads for routine, difficult, and shoulder dystocia deliveries. *Am J Obstet Gynecol* 1994;171:1621–7.

21. Benjamin K. Distinguishing physical characteristics and management of brachial plexus injuries. *Adv Neonatal Care* 2005;5:240–51.

Further reading

Crofts JF, Bartlett C, Ellis D, Hunt LP, Fox R, Draycott TS. Management of shoulder dystocia: skill retension 6 and 12 months after training. *Obstet Gynecol* 2007;110:1069–74.

Crofts JF, Bartlett C, Ellis D, Hunt LP, Fox R, Draycott TS. Training for shoulder dystocia: a trial of simulation using low-fidelity and high-fidelity mannequins. *Obstet Gynecol* 2006;108:1477–85.

Crofts JF, Ellis D, James M, Hunt LP, Fox R, Draycott TS. Pattern and degree of forces applied during simulation of shoulder dystocia. *Am J Obstet Gynecol* 2007;197:el-1–6.

Deering S, Poggi S, Macedonia C, Gherman R, Satin AJ. Improving resident competency in the management of shoulder dystocia with simulation training. *Obstet Gynecol* 2004;103:1224–8.

Module 8
Cord prolapse

Key learning points

- To recognise the risk factors for cord prolapse.
- To call for help.
- To perform manoeuvres to reduce pressure on the cord.
- To communicate effectively with the woman and the team and debrief.
- The importance of detailed contemporaneous documentation.

Common difficulties observed in training drills

- Recognition in the absence of external cord.
- Inappropriate handling of the cord.
- Moving woman in knee-to-chest position.
- Not calling appropriate help (anaesthetist, neonatal registrar).
- Difficulties with equipment for bladder filling.
- Not taking cord gases after delivery.

Introduction

Cord presentation is the presence of one or more loops of umbilical cord between the fetal presenting part and the cervix, with membranes intact. Cord prolapse has been defined as the descent of the umbilical cord through the cervix alongside (occult) or past the presenting part (overt) with ruptured membranes.

The incidence of umbilical cord prolapse ranges from 0.1–0.6% of all births.[1,2,3] In breech presentations it is just above 1%.[4]

Risk factors

Prior reports have suggested that conditions which result in a poor fit of the fetus in the maternal pelvis or cervix during delivery increase the risk of cord prolapse. A retrospective study of 132 consecutive cases of cord prolapse found there was a four-fold increase with preterm pregnancies. Risk factors (Box 8.1) should raise awareness but, inevitably, the possibility of cord prolapse occurring remains extremely unpredictable.

Box 8.1. Risk factors associated with cord prolapse	
General	**Procedure related**
Low birth weight < 2.5 kg	Artificial rupture of membranes
Prematurity < 37 weeks	External cephalic version
Polyhydramnios	Internal podalic version
Malpresentation (e.g. breech presentation, transverse lie)	Stabilising induction of labour
	Applying fetal scalp electrode
High presenting part	Rotational instrumental delivery
Fetal congenital anomalies	
Multiparity	
Second twin	

Perinatal complications

The perinatal mortality rate associated with umbilical cord prolapse remains high (approximately 9%) but has fallen over recent years. One study reported a rate of 91/1000.[2] The cause of death for infants born after umbilical cord prolapse now seems to be related more to the complications of prematurity and low birth weight than to intrapartum asphyxia itself.[2,5]

The fall in perinatal mortality may be due to the more rapid and frequent use of caesarean section once prolapsed cord has been diagnosed. However, given the association between umbilical cord prolapse and preterm birth, improvements in neonatal intensive care are probably as important.[4,6]

Evidence suggests that the interval between diagnosis and delivery is significantly related to stillbirth and neonatal death. Clearly, this means that when umbilical cord prolapse occurs out of hospital it carries a worse prognosis. Early diagnosis is important and continuous EFM may aid diagnosis (for example, performing a vaginal examination after a bradycardia auscultated).[2,7]

Initial management of cord prolapse

An outline for the management of cord prolapse is shown in Figure 8.1. This is described in detail in the next section.

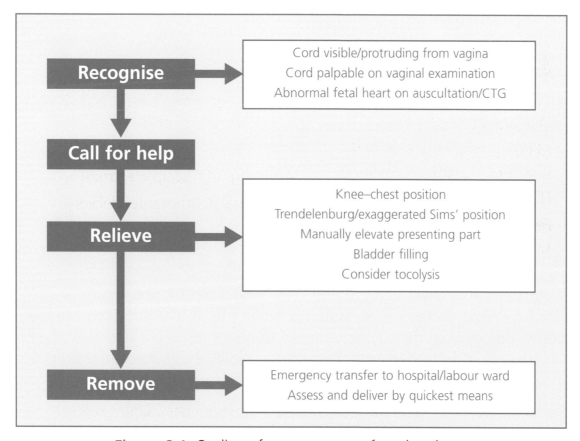

Figure 8.1. Outline of management of cord prolapse

RECOGNISE – cord prolapse

The cord may be visible at the vulva or may have prolapsed out of the vagina or it may be found on vaginal examination. A combination of any of the risk factors listed in Box 8.1 and an abnormal fetal heart rate/CTG should heighten awareness of possible occult cord prolapse.

Call for help

If you are in hospital, activate the emergency buzzer to summon assistance and emergency bleep key personnel:

- obstetric registrar
- anaesthetic registrar
- senior labour ward midwife
- experienced neonatologist/resuscitation team.

Alert the consultant obstetrician and consultant anaesthetist and alert theatre staff to prepare for possible category 1 caesarean section. Note the time of emergency calls and time of arrival of staff.

If a cord prolapse occurs at home, the community midwife should call the paramedic ambulance to attend immediately.

RELIEVE – cord compression

Relieve cord compression by elevation of the presenting part. Traditionally, management of umbilical cord prolapse has recommended knee–chest position, as shown in Figure 8.2. However, this position is unsuitable for transportation and therefore Trendelenberg or exaggerated Sim's position (left-lateral with a pillow under left hip) may be used instead.

If cord prolapse is recognised at the time of rupture of membranes, the fingers should be kept within the vagina to elevate the presenting part, thus reducing compression of the cord, particularly during contractions.

If an oxytocin infusion is in progress, this should be stopped immediately. The fetal heart should be monitored continuously. If the umbilical cord has prolapsed out from the vagina, attempt to gently replace it back into the vagina with minimal handling. There is no evidence to support the practice of covering the cord with sterile gauze soaked in warm, physiological saline.

Some authors have also suggested the use of tocolysis, such as terbutaline 0.25 mg subcutaneously, to inhibit uterine contractions.[8,9]

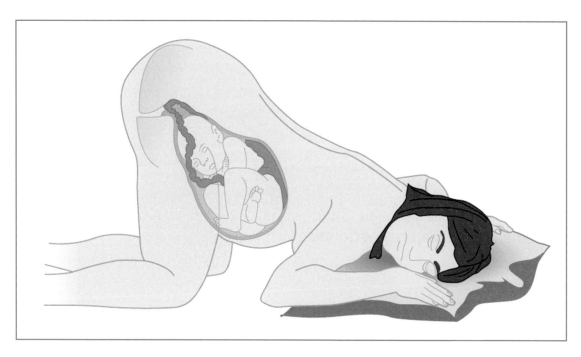

Figure 8.2. Knee-chest position to relieve pressure on cord

Bladder filling

If the decision-to-delivery interval is likely to be prolonged, particularly if it involves ambulance transfer, elevation of the presenting part by bladder filling may be considered.

Bladder filling was first proposed by Vago in 1970,[10] as a method of relieving pressure on the umbilical cord. Bladder filling raises the presenting part of the fetus off the compressed cord for an extended period of time, thereby eliminating the need for an examiner's fingers to displace the presenting part.[10,11]

A 16-gauge Foley catheter is placed into the urinary bladder. The bladder is filled via the catheter with physiological (0.9%) saline using an intravenous blood infusion set. The catheter should be clamped once 500–750 ml has been instilled. It is essential to empty the bladder again just before any method of delivery is attempted.

Filling the bladder may also decrease or inhibit uterine contractions.

Assessment of fetal wellbeing

Continuous EFM should be performed so that the wellbeing of the baby can be constantly assessed. If there is no audible fetal heart and the umbilical cord is not pulsating, an ultrasound scan should be performed. Driscoll *et al.*[12] demonstrated the importance of prompt ultrasound assessment in a patient presenting with the absence of cord pulsation and inaudible fetal heart tones. They found that fetal heart movements could be visualised, even in the absence of cord pulsation and inaudible heart tones.

REMOVE – transport and deliver

The risks to perinatal mortality and morbidity mean that cord prolapse should be managed in a unit with full anaesthetic and neonatal services. If cord prolapse occurs away from the delivery suite, immediate transfer to the labour ward is essential. Clearly, good communication is required so that appropriate members of staff are ready to receive the mother on arrival and theatre should be on standby.

If there is no intravenous access, site a wide-bore intravenous cannulae (14/16-gauge) and take blood for group and save and full blood count.

ASSESSMENT FOR DELIVERY

- If the cervix is fully dilated without signs of fetal compromise, consider assisted vaginal delivery.
- If the cervix is not fully dilated and there are signs of fetal compromise, prepare for category 1 caesarean section (in the case of a second twin or multiparity, with severe CTG abnormalities, a ventouse extraction may be considered by experienced operators at 9 cm dilatation. In these cases, continuous fetal monitoring is important).
- If the cervix is not fully dilated without signs of fetal compromise, consider a category 2 caesarean section.

Umbilical cord prolapse at full dilatation with a live viable fetus can be managed by instrumental delivery providing the head is in the pelvis and less than 1/5 palpable per abdomen.

If vaginal delivery is not possible and the fetus is viable then preparations for emergency caesarean section should be made.[11] If there is evidence of fetal compromise then a category 1 caesarean section should be planned but if there is no obvious fetal compromise then a category 2 caesarean section may be appropriate.

The method of anaesthesia (general, spinal, epidural top-up) should be made, with consideration to the fetal condition. Optimal communication is required between the obstetricians and anaesthetists.

Parents

Cord prolapse is a frightening experience for the parents. It is important to tell the parents what is happening and to give the mother clear instructions. The parents will need support and debriefing. Clinicians should be encouraged to visit the parents the following day and subsequently, if required, to discuss events, answer any questions and address concerns.

Key points

- Cord prolapse is a life threatening situation for the baby.
- Once a cord prolapse is recognised:
  - **relieve** the pressure on the cord.
  - **remove** the mother to appropriate place of delivery.
  - **remove** the baby by the safest and most expedient means.
- Document your actions clearly and legibly.
- Discuss events with the parents.

References

1. Critchlow CW, Leet TL, Benedetti TJ, Daling JR. Risk factors and infant outcomes associated with umbilical cord prolapse: a population-based case-control study among births in Washington State. *Am J Obstet Gynecol* 1994;170:613–18.

2. Murphy DJ, MacKenzie IZ. The mortality and morbidity associated with umbilical cord prolapse. *Br J Obstet Gynaecol* 1995;102:826–3.

3. Lin MG. Umbilical cord prolapse. *Obstet Gynecol Surv* 2006;61:269–77.

4. Panter KR, Hannah ME. Umbilical cord prolapse: so far so good? *Lancet* 1996;347:74.

5. Yla-Outinen A, Heinonen PK, Tuimala R. Predisposing and risk factors of umbilical cord prolapse. *Acta Obstet Gynecol Scand* 1985;64:567–70.

6. Ferrara TB, Hoekstra RE, Gaziano E, Knox GE, Couser RJ, Fangman JJ. Changing outcome of extremely premature infants (< 26 weeks gestation and < 750 g): survival and follow up at a tertiary centre. *Am J Obstet Gynecol* 1989;161:1114–8.

7. Koonings PP, Paul RH, Campbell K. Umbilical cord prolapse a contemporary look. *J Reprod Med* 1990;35:690–2.

8. Gruese ME, Prickett SA. Nursing management of umbilical cord prolapse. *J Obstet Gynecol* 1993;107:311–15.

9. Katz Z, Shoham Z, Lancet M, Blickstein I, Mogilner BM, Zalel Y. Management of labor with umbilical cord prolapse: a 5 year study. *Obstet Gynecol* 1994;94:278–81.

10. Vago T. Prolapse of the umbilical cord. A method of management. *Am J Obstet Gynecol* 1970;107:967–9.

11. Caspi E, Lotan Y, Schreyer P. Prolapse of the cord: reduction of perinatal mortality by bladder instillation and caesarean section. *Isr J Med Sci* 1983;19:541–5.

12. Driscoll JA, Sadan O, Van Gelderen CJ, Holloway GA. Cord prolapse: can we save more babies? *Br J Obstet Gynaecol* 1987;94:594–5.

Further reading

Barrett JM. Funic reduction for the management of umbilical cord prolapse. *Am J Obstet Gynecol* 1991;165:654–7.

Chetty RM, Moodley J. *S Afr Med J* 1980;57:128–9.

Fenton AN, d'Esopo DA. Prolapse of the cord during labor. *Am J Obstet Gynecol* 1951;62:52–64.

Mesleh T, Sultan M, Sabagh T, Algwiser A. Umbilical cord prolapse. *J Obstet Gynecol* 1993;13:24–8.

Royal College of Obstetricians and Gynaecologists. *Umbilical Cord Prolapse.* Green-top Guideline No. 50. London: RCOG;2008 [www.rcog.org.uk/index.asp?PageID=2384].

Tchabo JG. The use of the contact hysteroscope in the diagnosis of cord prolapse. *Int Surg* 1988;43:129–32.

Module 9
Vaginal breech

Key learning points

- The importance of continuous electronic fetal monitoring in labour (even if decision has been made to perform a caesarean section).
- Confirmation of full dilatation.
- Await visualisation of the breech at the perineum before encouraging active pushing.
- Limited intervention is the key – avoid traction.

Common difficulties observed in training drills

- Reluctance to allow the breech to descend without intervention.
- Premature commencement of assisted breech manoeuvres.
- Pressure on non-bony prominences when handling the baby.

Introduction

The incidence of breech presentation in the UK is 3–4% at term, although it is much higher earlier in pregnancy (for example, at 28 weeks of gestation 20% of babies are breech presentation). It is associated with a higher perinatal morbidity and mortality than cephalic presentation owing to prematurity, congenital malformations, birth asphyxia and trauma.[1] These risk factors should inform antenatal, intrapartum and neonatal management.

Definition

Breech presentation is where the presenting part of the fetus is the buttocks or feet; the breech can be extended, flexed or footling (Figure 9.1).

Predisposing factors

Factors that predispose to a breech presentation are listed in Box 9.1.

Box 9.1. Factors associated with breech presentation

Previous term breech presentation	Uterine anomalies
Premature labour	Pelvic tumour or fibroids
High parity	Placenta praevia
Multiple pregnancy	Hydrocephaly/anencephaly
Polyhydramnios	Fetal neuromuscular disorders
Oligohydramnios	Fetal head and neck tumours

The rate of vaginal breech delivery has declined over recent years from 1.2% in 1980 to 0.3% in 2001 and has continued to decline as a result of the Term Breech Trial.[2-4] This study compared outcomes after planned vaginal and planned caesarean births for breech presentation and demonstrated a significant reduction in perinatal morbidity and mortality in the planned caesarean group (reduction in mortality of 75%). In addition, there was no significant increase in maternal morbidity or mortality with planned caesarean births. However, the 2-year follow-up data from the trial have not demonstrated any statistically significant differences in neurodevelopment between the two groups, questioning whether the long-term benefits of planned caesarean birth for breech presentation outweighs the risks.

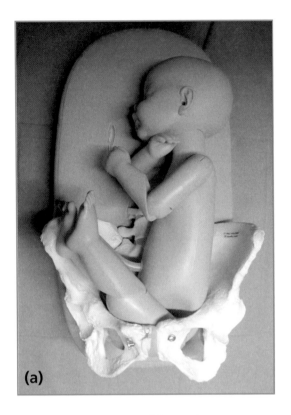

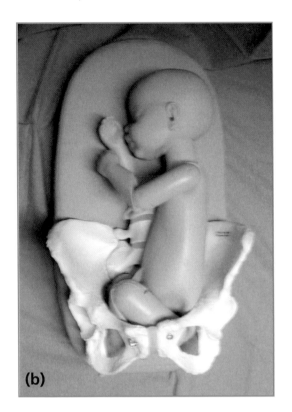

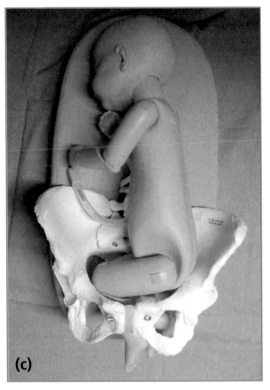

Figure 9.1. Types of breech presentation (clockwise): (a) extended (65%) hips flexed, knees extended; (b) flexed (10%) hips flexed, knees flexed but feet not below the buttocks; (c) footling (25%) feet or knees are lowest (either single or double footling)

The optimum mode of delivery for women in advanced labour, preterm breech delivery and breech presentation in the second twin remains unclear, as the Term Breech Trial did not investigate these factors.

It is important that practitioners maintain and update their skills in assisting vaginal breech deliveries. Their skills may be required because of maternal choice or for other reasons such as a breech presentation of the second twin, an unexpected breech presentation in advanced labour or for a breech preterm birth. RCOG recommendations for mode of delivery are shown in Box 9.2.

Box 9.2. Summary of RCOG recommendations regarding mode of delivery in breech presentation (adapted from RCOG Green-top Guideline No.20b)[1]

- Neonatal morbidity and mortality is reduced by planned caesarean section in breech presentation at term.
- There is no evidence that caesarean section for the first or second twin (breech presentation) is more beneficial.
- There is no evidence that caesarean section for a preterm breech is more beneficial.
- There is no evidence that caesarean section for a labouring breech is more beneficial.
- There is no evidence to support external cephalic version (ECV) in preterm breech.
- There is no evidence of long-term benefit in perinatal outcome for a breech presentation delivered by elective caesarean section.

Management of vaginal breech delivery

Types of vaginal breech delivery

Spontaneous breech delivery:	The fetus is allowed to deliver without assistance or manipulation. This accounts for a small proportion of deliveries, most of which are very preterm.
Assisted breech delivery:	The most common method of vaginal breech delivery. Recognised manoeuvres are used to assist delivery as and when required.
Total breech extraction:	Mainly reserved for delivery of the non-cephalic second twin. It involves grasping one or both of the fetal feet from the uterine cavity and bringing

them down through the vagina, before continuing with the manoeuvres used in an assisted breech delivery. This should not be attempted in singleton pregnancies, as it is associated with a high rate of birth injury (25%) and mortality (10%).

Management of the first stage of labour

It is recommended that a vaginal breech birth should take place in a hospital with facilities for emergency caesarean section. There is no systematic evidence available regarding the complications of breech birth outside the hospital setting.[1]

Preparation

Inform the senior midwife, senior obstetrician, anaesthetist and theatre staff of admission and ensure key members of staff are introduced to the parents.

Discuss the mode of delivery again with the woman and ensure that she still wishes to opt for a vaginal breech birth. Discuss analgesia early in the process. There is no evidence that epidural anaesthesia is essential and it should not be routinely advised. A woman should have a choice of analgesia during breech labour and birth.[1] Explain all delivery techniques and the necessity for the presence of a neonatologist at delivery.

Establish intravenous access and take blood for full blood count and group and save.

The delivery room and neonatal resuscitation equipment should be prepared. Ensure that prerequisites for an assisted vaginal delivery are present: operative delivery pack, forceps, lithotomy supports.

Electronic fetal monitoring

Owing to the greater risks of perinatal morbidity and mortality, continuous EFM should be offered and recommended to women with a breech presentation throughout labour and delivery. The seventh CESDI annual report reviewed 56 singleton breech deliveries and found clinical evidence of hypoxia before delivery in all but one case.[2] The report concluded that: 'The assessments and decisions made by health professionals, during labour, in particular those regarding intrapartum fetal surveillance, were the critical factors in the avoidable deaths'.

A fetal scalp electrode can be placed on the fetal buttock if required but fetal blood sampling is not recommended.[5]

Labour progress

Labour augmentation with oxytocin is not recommended. Amniotomy should be performed with caution and may be necessary to allow for the use of internal fetal heart rate monitoring.

Once spontaneous rupture of the membranes occurs, a vaginal examination should be performed to exclude a cord prolapse.

Management of the second stage of labour

If there is delay in the descent of the breech at any point in the second stage of labour, a caesarean section should be considered, as this may be a sign of relative fetopelvic disproportion.[1]

A breech delivery should be undertaken or supervised by a practitioner with adequate experience and skills in the delivery techniques required for a breech birth. The attendants should include a senior midwife, obstetrician and neonatologist (the senior midwife may also have valuable experience of vaginal breech deliveries). An anaesthetist should be present on the labour ward at the time of delivery and theatre staff should be on stand-by.

Women should be advised that, as most experience with vaginal breech birth is with the mother in the lithotomy position, this should be the position recommended for delivery.[1] Consider a pudendal block if there is no epidural analgesia. Once the breech is visible at the perineum, active pushing should be encouraged.

> **Remember: limited operator intervention is key**

Vaginal breech delivery: assisted manoeuvres

- An episiotomy should only be performed when indicated to facilitate the delivery.[1]
- When handling the baby, ensure that support is provided over the bony prominences so that the risk of soft tissue internal injury is reduced.
- Spontaneous delivery of the limbs and trunk is preferable (Figure 9.2a) but the legs may need to be released by applying pressure to the popliteal fossae (Figure 9.2b).

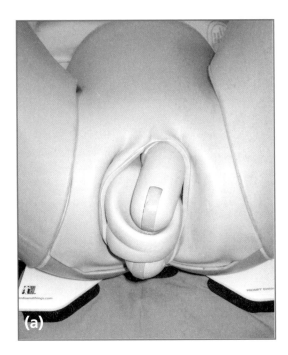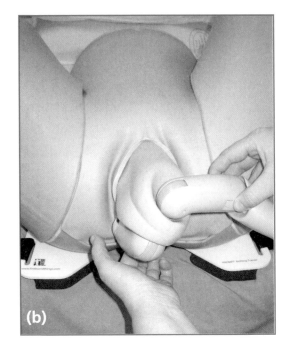

Figure 9.2. Delivery of fetal legs

- Consider correcting the position of the buttocks to sacroanterior, if required.
- Avoid handling the umbilical cord as it may spasm.
- Allow spontaneous delivery until the scapulae are visible.
- If the arms do not deliver spontaneously, use the Lovsett's manoeuvre, as shown in Figure 9.3.

Engagement in the pelvis of the aftercoming head

Allow the baby to hang until the nape of the neck is visible; the head can then be delivered. If the head does not deliver spontaneously, an assistant may apply supra pubic pressure to assist flexion of the head.

Mauriceau-Smellie-Veit manoeuvre

The Mauriceau-Smellie-Veit manoeuvre may be required for delivery of the aftercoming head (Figure 9.4). When using this manoeuvre, the baby's body should be supported with your arm. The first and third finger of your hand should be placed on the cheekbones (note that the middle finger is **no longer** placed in the fetal mouth as fetal injury has been reported). With the other hand, gentle traction should be applied simultaneously to the shoulders, using two fingers to flex the occiput (Figure 9.5).

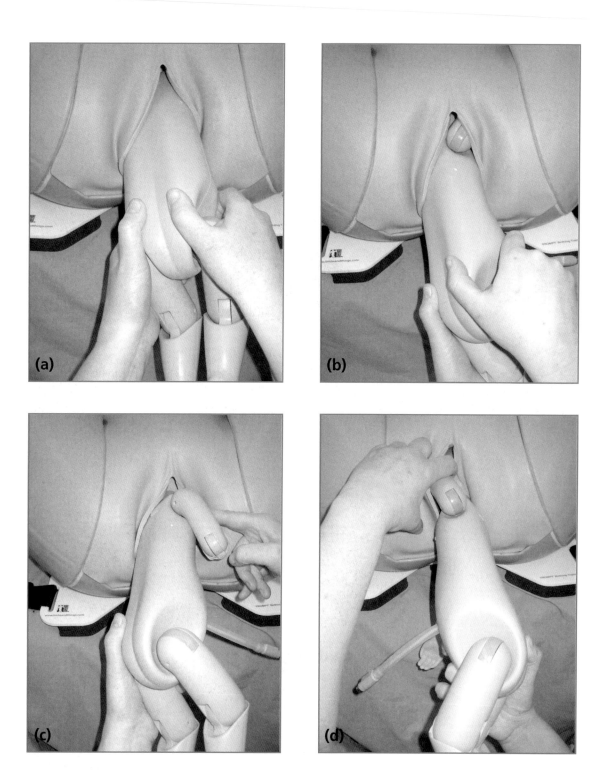

Figure 9.3. Lovsett's manoeuvre: (a) Gently hold the baby over the bony prominences of the hips and turn half a circle. Keep the back uppermost and simultaneously apply downward traction; (b) The lateral arm is now anterior and can be delivered under the public arch; (c) Place one or two fingers on the upper part of the arm and draw it down over the chest as the elbow is flexed and sweep over the face; (d) Turn the baby back half a circle to deliver the second arm. Keep the back uppermost and simultaneously apply downward traction and deliver the second arm under the public arch

Figure 9.4. The Mauriceau-Smellie-Veit manoeuvre for delivery of the aftercoming head

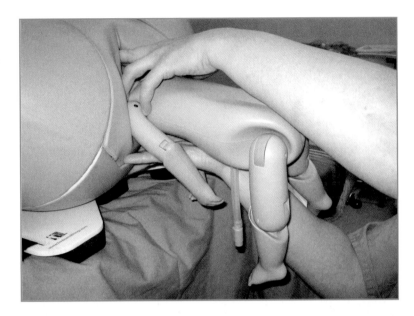

Figure 9.5. Flexion and delivery of the fetal head using the Mauriceau-Smellie-Veit manoeuvre

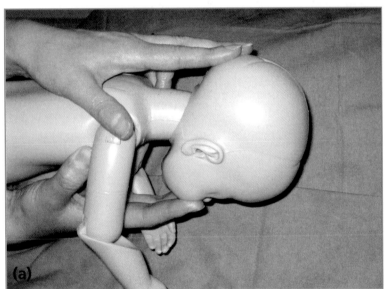

(a)

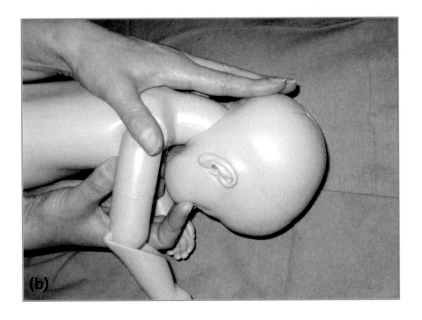

(b)

Burns-Marshall technique

Another way of delivering the head is to raise the body vertically and have an assistant hold the baby's feet (Burns-Marshall technique). Sometimes, this will promote spontaneous delivery of the head (Figure 9.6).

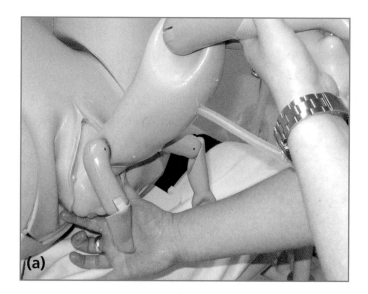

Figure 9.6. The Burns–Marshall technique for delivering the head

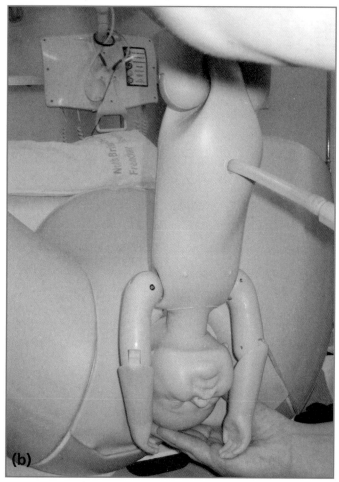

(a)

(b)

Forceps delivery of the head

Alternatively, the fetal head can be delivered with the aid of forceps. An assistant should hold the baby and the forceps should be applied from underneath the fetal body. The axis of traction should aim to flex the head (Figure 9.7). There is debate over which type of forceps should be used for this procedure: Kielland, Rhodes' and Wrigley's forceps have all been reported.

There is no experimental evidence to indicate which of the above techniques is preferable and previous experience of the practitioner may be an important factor in the decision as to which method is chosen. However, concern has been expressed about the risks of the Burns-Marshall method if used incorrectly, as it may lead to over-extension of the baby's neck.[1]

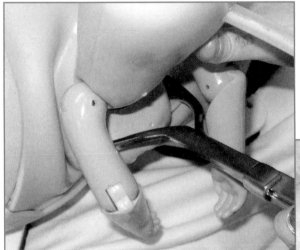

Figure 9.7.
Kielland forceps
delivery of the head

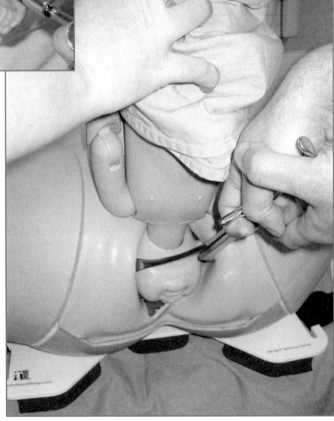

Figure 9.8.
Nuchal arm

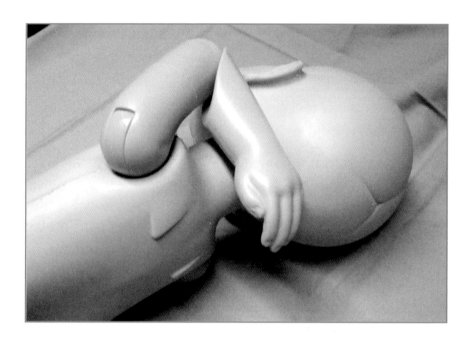

Complications and potential solutions

Failure to deliver the aftercoming head

If conservative methods fail to deliver the head then symphysiotomy or caesarean section should be performed. There have been successful deliveries described by both symphysiotomy and rapid caesarean section when attempts to deliver the aftercoming head have failed.[1]

Head entrapment during a preterm breech delivery

The major cause of head entrapment is the delivery of the preterm fetal trunk through an incompletely dilated cervix. In this situation, the cervix can be incised to release the head. The incisions should be made at 10 and 2 o'clock, to avoid the cervical neurovascular bundles which run laterally into the cervix. Care should be taken as extension into the lower segment of the uterus can occur. Similar rates of head entrapment have been described for vaginal and abdominal delivery.[6]

Nuchal arms

This is when one or both of the arms is extended and trapped behind the fetal head, complicating up to 5% of breech deliveries (Figure 9.8). It may be caused by early traction on a breech, which should be avoided. Twenty-five percent of cases result in neonatal trauma, such as brachial plexus injuries.

To deliver nuchal arms, the fetal trunk must be rotated to enable the fetal face to turn towards the maternal symphysis pubis. This reduces the tension on the arm and allows delivery using Lovsett's manoeuvre.

Cord prolapse

This is more common with footling breech presentations (10–25%), which is why caesarean section is strongly recommended. The most important factor with cord prolapse is prevention. Amniotomy should only be undertaken with caution. The management of cord prolapse is outlined in **Module 8**.

Fetal risks associated with vaginal breech birth

Box 9.3 lists the risks associated with a vaginal breech birth. CESDI highlighted that the highest risk group were those unexpected breech presentations which were confirmed for the first time during labour.[2]

Box 9.3. Fetal risks associated with vaginal breech birth
Intrapartum death
Intracranial haemorrhage
Brachial plexus injury
Rupture of the liver, kidney or spleen
Dislocation of the neck, shoulder or hip
Fractured clavicle, humerus or femur
Cord prolapse

References

1. Royal College of Obstetricians and Gynaecologists. *The Management of Breech Presentation*. Green-top Guideline No. 20b. London: RCOG; 2006.
2. Confidential Enquiry into Stillbirths and Deaths in Infancy. *7th Annual Report*. London: Maternal and Child Health Research Consortium; 2000.
3. Department of Health (2002) NHS Maternity Statistics, England: 2001–02. Bulletin 2003/09 [www.dh.gov.uk/en/Publicationsandstatistics/Statistics/StatisticalWorkAreas/Statisticalhealthcare/DH_4086520].

4. Hannah ME, Hannah WJ, Hewson SA, Hodnett ED, Saigal S, Willan AR, *et al*. Planned caesarean section versus planned vaginal birth for breech presentation at term: a randomised multicentre trial. *Lancet* 2002;356:1375–83.

5. National Collaborating Centre for Women's and Children's Health. *Intrapartum Care: care of healthy women and their babies during childbirth. Clinical guideline*. London: NCC-WCH; 2007.

6. Robertson PA, Foran CM, Croughan-Minihane MS, Kilpatrick SJ. Head entrapment and neonatal outcome by mode of delivery in breech deliveries from 28 to 36 weeks of gestation. *Am J Obstet Gynecol* 1996;174:1742–7.

Further reading

James DK, Steer PJ, Weiner CP, Gonik B. *High Risk Pregnancy*. 2nd ed. London: WB Saunders; 1999.

Module 10
Basic newborn resuscitation

Key learning points

- To develop and practice a structured approach to the skills required in neonatal resuscitation.
- To understand the causes of respiratory and cardiac arrest in the neonate and show an awareness of problems due to maternal obstetric history.
- To understand the importance of calling for help early.
- To communicate effectively to the parents and the neonatal team.
- To complete accurate documentation.

Difficulties observed in previous neonatal resuscitation drills

- Poor thermal care during resuscitation, especially in preterm infants.
- Failure to open infant's airway adequately, usually due to overextension of the neck.
- Loss of effective airway maintenance, particularly when conducting simultaneous cardiac compressions.
- Performing chest compressions too slowly.

Introduction

This module provides an outline of the process of basic newborn resuscitation but is not intended to be a complete guide. Further information is available from the Resuscitation Council (UK) publications, *Newborn Life Support: Resuscitation at Birth* and the *Resuscitation Guidelines 2005*.[1,2]

Background

All neonates experience a degree of hypoxia during the process of labour and delivery, with respiratory exchange being interrupted for as long as 50–75 seconds with each contraction throughout labour. While most healthy babies tolerate this well, some do not and may require additional help to establish normal breathing once born.[1]

Newborn babies are designed to undertake the stress of labour and the neonate's brain can withstand much longer periods without oxygen than an adult brain. In addition, a neonate's heart can continue to beat effectively for 20 minutes or more without lung aeration, even after the reserve system of gasping has ceased. Therefore, the primary aim of newborn resuscitation is inflation of the lungs with air or oxygen, so that the still functioning circulation can then pump oxygenated blood to and from the heart to initiate recovery.[1]

Physiology of neonatal hypoxia

There are two centres in the brain that are responsible for the control of respiration; one is a higher centre.

If the hypoxic insult to the infant is sufficient, the fetus' breathing movements in utero become deeper and more rapid and eventually cease as the centres responsible for controlling them are unable to function due to lack of oxygen. This is known as the 'primary apnoea' phase.[1]

Once the fetus enters 'primary apnoea', the heart rate falls to about half its usual rate as the heart muscle switches from using aerobic to the less efficient anaerobic metabolism. Lactic acid build-up from anaerobic metabolism causes the fetus to become acidotic and the circulation is diverted away from non-essential organs.

After a variable length of time of continuing hypoxia, unconscious gasping activity is initiated. The fetus produces a shuddering, whole-body gasp at an approximate rate of 12 breaths/minute.[3] If these gasps fail to aerate the fetal lungs then breathing ceases all together, leading to secondary or 'terminal apnoea'. At this point, as the fetus becomes increasingly acidotic, the heart begins to fail. If there is no effective intervention at this stage then the baby will die and may even die despite treatment.[1] The whole process probably takes about 20 minutes in a newborn baby.[4]

While the heart continues to beat, the most important part of neonatal resuscitation is aerating the lungs. This will enable oxygenation of the heart and, hence, the brain and its respiratory centres. Unfortunately, it is not possible to tell at the time of birth whether a baby who is not breathing is in primary apnoea and about to gasp or is in the terminal apnoea phase. However, in most cases, once air or oxygen enters the lungs, the infant will recover quickly and normal breathing will begin. A few may require cardiac massage, but usually for only a short period of time.[1]

A few babies born at the point of terminal apnoea, as mentioned previously, will die without intervention and may die despite it. In addition to ventilation and cardiac massage, drugs may be required to restore the circulation. By this stage, a senior neonatologist should be in attendance and will lead the resuscitation. If drugs are required, then generally the outlook is poor for the infant.

Preparation of resuscitation equipment

Successful resuscitation is dependent on forward planning. Before any birth, it is the responsibility of the midwife and/or neonatologist to prepare and check resuscitation equipment.

It is important to check and prepare:

- clock and light
- oxygen and suction (cylinders full and suction tubing attached)
- heater (resuscitaire) and towels (pre-warmed)
- equipment for administering oxygen (bag/valve mask and appropriate sized mask, T-piece tubing)
- neonatal laryngoscopes (correct sized blades and light working)
- notes for documentation.

When preparing for a birth, consider the woman's obstetric history and call the neonatal team and/or an additional midwife to be present in advance, if indicated.

It is important to explain to the parents that a neonatologist has been called and to keep them informed of the situation.

Assessment and resuscitation

As with any emergency, it is important to call for help early. An outline of basic newborn resuscitation is shown in Figure 10.1 but this is not intended to be a complete guide. Further information is available from the Resuscitation Council UK.[1,2]

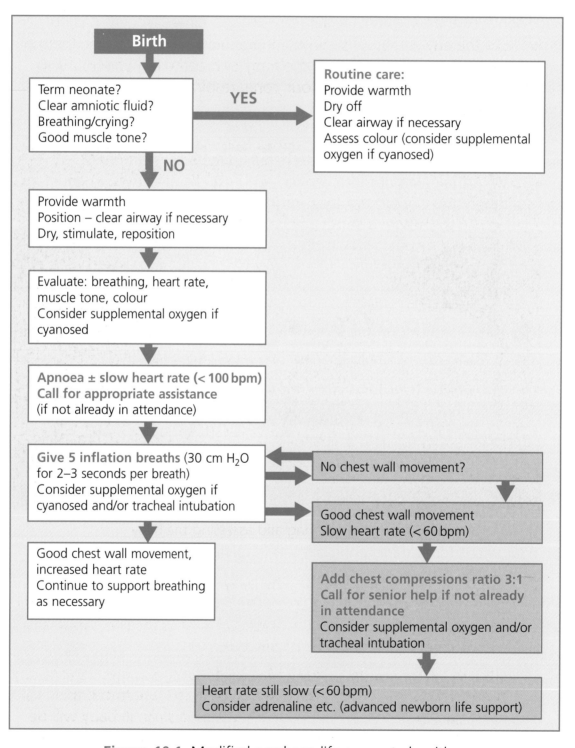

Figure 10.1. Modified newborn life support algorithm

1. Warmth and assessment at birth

Newborn babies have a large surface area to body ratio and are wet from liquor etc. at birth. They therefore lose heat very rapidly, and if anoxic and/or small, can quickly become hypothermic.[5]

■ Start the clock and note the time of delivery

■ Check that the cord is securely clamped.

■ Remove the any wet towels and then wrap in warm dry towels. Drying the baby will not only stimulate the baby to breathe but will also give time for a full assessment of colour, tone, respiratory effort and heart rate (Figure 10.2).

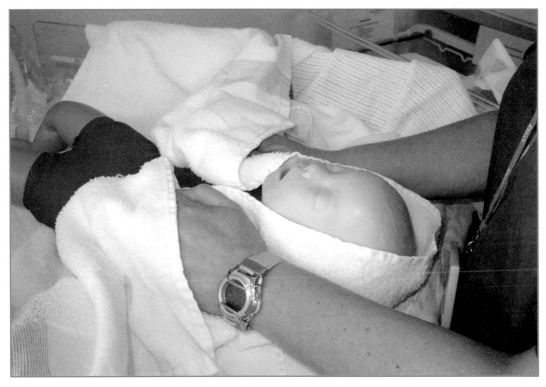

Figure 10.2. Drying and assessing the baby

■ If less than 31 weeks of gestation, the baby should be placed, without drying, in a food-grade plastic bag under a radiant heater, exposing only their face, during resuscitation and stabilisation at birth. The bag is very effective at keeping the preterm infant warm.

■ A healthy baby may be born blue but should have good muscle tone, cry within a few seconds of delivery, have a good heart rate (more than 100 bpm) and quickly become pink, within 1–2 minutes. An ill baby will be pale and floppy at birth, with absent breathing and a slow heart rate.

2. Airway

Most babies at birth have a prominent occiput which causes them to flex their neck if placed flat on their backs; this in turn blocks off their airway. To avoid this happening, the baby should be placed on his back with his head held in a neutral position, by placing some support under the shoulders (Figure 10.3).

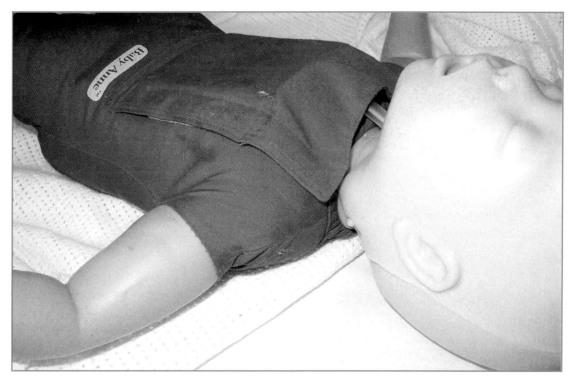

Figure 10.3. Head in neutral position with shoulders suspended

If the baby is very floppy then a chin lift or jaw thrust may also be necessary to keep the airway open (Figure 10.4).

If an obstruction is suspected, then suction should only be performed under direct vision with a laryngoscope.

3. Breathing

If the baby is not breathing adequately by about 90 seconds, then five inflation breaths should be given. It is important that the correct size mask is used: covering the chin, but not over the eyes or squeezing the nose (Figure 10.5). The baby's lungs are filled with fluid at birth, so the inflation breaths will force out the fluid and fill the lungs with air or oxygen. The pressure required to initially inflate the lungs is equivalent to 30 cm of water for 2–3 seconds/breath.[1]

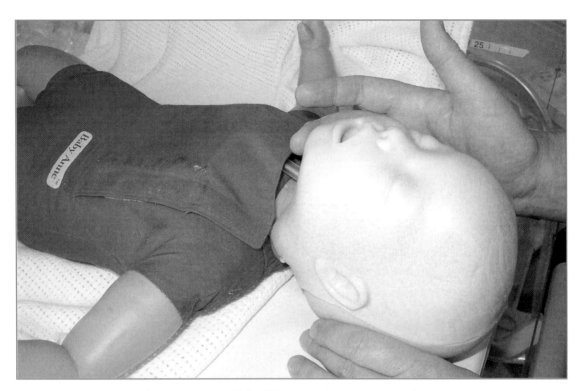

Figure 10.4. Chin lift to maintain open airway

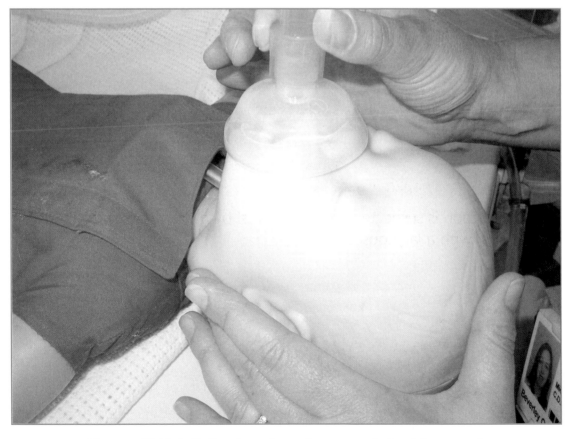

Figure 10.5. Inflation breaths using correct-sized face mask

If the lungs have been effectively inflated, passive movements of the chest wall will be visible and the heart rate should also increase, as oxygenated blood reaches the heart. If the heart rate increases but the baby does not start breathing on his own, then regular ventilation breaths at a rate of about 30–40/minute should be continued until the baby begins to breathe for himself.

If the heart rate does not increase following inflation breaths, it may be because the baby needs more than lung aeration. However, the most likely cause is that the lungs have not been aerated effectively. Therefore, go back to the start and check the airway, making sure that the baby's head is in the neutral position with a jaw thrust if necessary, and that there is no obstruction in the oropharynx. If the chest wall still does not move, request assistance in maintaining the airway and consider using a Guedel.

If the heart rate remains slow or is absent despite five good inflation breaths with passive chest movement, chest compressions are needed and senior neonatal support should be requested.

4. Chest compression/circulation

Almost all babies needing resuscitation at birth will respond successfully to lung inflation, with a rise in heart rate proceeding rapidly to normal breathing. However, in some cases chest compression is necessary.

It is important that chest compression should only be commenced, when it is certain that the lungs have been successfully inflated.

Senior neonatal support should be summoned if not already in attendance.

The most efficient way to perform chest compressions in an infant is to grip the chest with both hands, with both thumbs pressing on the lower third of the sternum, just below the nipple line, with the fingers over the spine at the back (Figure 10.6).

Compress the chest quickly and firmly to a depth of about one-third of the distance from the chest to the spine.

The ratio of compressions to breaths recommended in a newborn infant are 3:1 to achieve 90 compressions and 30 breaths in 1 minute .

Allow enough time between compressions for oxygenated blood to flow from the lungs to the heart at a rate of approximately 140 compressions/minute. Ensure that the chest is inflating with each ventilation breath.

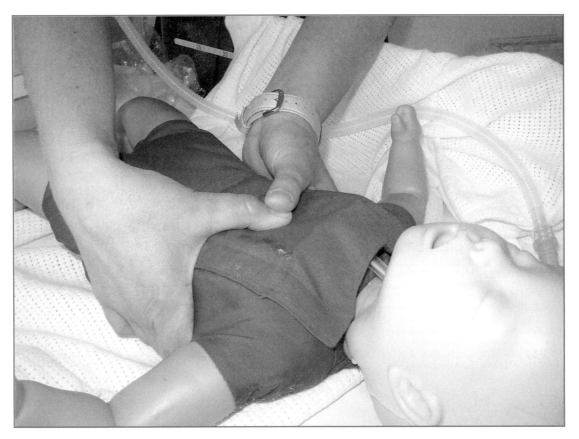

Figure 10.6. Positioning for chest compressions

In a very small number of babies, lung inflation and chest compressions will not be sufficient to generate an effective circulation and, in such circumstances, drugs may be required.

5. Emergency drugs

Emergency drugs are only needed if there is no significant circulatory response despite effective ventilation and chest compressions. A senior neonatologist should be in attendance at this stage and it is their responsibility to intubate the infant and administer medication.

6. Special circumstances

Meconium at delivery

There is no evidence that suctioning meconium from the nose and mouth of the infant while the head is still on the perineum prevents meconium aspiration and so this practice is no longer recommended.[6]

In addition, attempting to remove meconium from the airways of a vigorously crying infant has also been proven to be ineffective at preventing meconium aspiration.[7] However, if a baby is born where thick meconium liquor is present and is unresponsive at birth, then the oropharynx should be suctioned to clear the meconium. If intubation skills are available, then the larynx and trachea can also be cleared, although it is acknowledged that there is no evidence of the effectiveness of this practice.

Naloxone

Babies affected by their mother having pethidine in labour normally cry immediately after delivery and then become apnoeic once dried, warm and comfortable.

Babies are most at risk when the mother has had repeated doses of pethidine less than 3 hours apart, when she has been given it intravenously or when the pethidine has been administered less than 3 hours before delivery.

Standard resuscitation is required immediately. Only when the infant has a secure airway, with lungs effectively aerated and its heart rate normal, is naloxone to be considered.

Dose: 200 micrograms or 0.5 ml of adult naloxone (Narcan®, Du Pont Pharmaceuticals) given intramuscularly in the infant's thigh. Smaller doses may be given but naloxone's action is short-lived, only a few hours if given intramuscularly, whereas the effect of pethidine in the infant can last for more than 24 hours.

Documentation

It is important that all actions are documented accurately and comprehensively in the appropriate case notes, particularly when resuscitation at birth has been necessary, as records may be carefully scrutinised many years later.

References

1. Resuscitation Council (UK). *Newborn Life Support: Resuscitation at Birth*. 2nd ed. London: Resuscitation Council; 2006.

2. Resuscitation Council (UK). *Resuscitation Guidelines 2005*. London: Resuscitation Council; 2005.

3. Dawes G. *Fetal and Neonatal Physiology*. Chicago: Year Book Publisher; 1968. Chapter 12: p. 141–59.

4. Hey, Kelly J. Gaseous exchange during endotracheal ventilation for asphyxia at birth. *J Obstet Gynaecol Br Commonw* 1968;75:414–23.

5. Dahm LS, James LS. Newborn temperature and calculated heat loss in the delivery room. *Pediatrics* 1972;49:504–13.

6. Vain NE, Szyld EG, Prudent LM, Wiswell TE, Aguilar AM, Vivas NI. Oropharyngeal and nasopharyngeal suctioning of meconium-stained neonates before delivery of their shoulders: multicentre, randomised controlled trial. *Lancet* 2004:364;597–602.

7. Wiswell TE, Gannon CM, Jacob J, Goldsmith L, Szyld E, Weiss K, *et al*. Delivery room management of the apparently vigorous meconium-stained neonate: results of the multicentre international collaborative trial. *Pediatrics* 2000;105:1–7.

Index